The Lord's Prayer in the Preacher's Life

The opening story is gripping. I was hooked; there was no way I could put down this book in a hurry! This is definitely not another "how to" book on preaching. Subtly, attention is drawn to an often neglected area – the preacher's life and character. The unknown sustaining work of the foundation and formation, of the personhood, the inner being of the preacher, is the fountain from where all sermons outflow. This book addresses this aspect of preaching.

Indeed, the adage "The medium is the message" is jarringly highlighted again and again. Oh it jolts and hurts, but we need to hear this more often than not if we are to fulfill our calling as preachers of the word.

The value of this book is not only the brilliant perspective on the life of the preacher from the Lord's Prayer, but it turns out to be a workbook. It encourages *meditatio*, which is absolutely necessary for a preacher's formation. Every chapter can become a holy moment – the exposition in this book creates that kind of ambience! This is a groundbreaking book – a must-have book!

Alongla Aier
Professor of English and Communication,
Oriental Theological Seminary, Nagaland, India

These profound meditations on the Lord's Prayer illustrated by incidents from the life of Christ can feed preachers with rich food that brings renewal to their lives.

Ajith Fernando
Teaching Director,
Youth for Christ, Sri Lanka

Becoming truly faithful preachers of the gospel does not happen overnight. Oh, one can experience a powerful "call to preach" in a moment – a call that can sustain us for the rest of our ministries. But becoming a truly faithful preacher of the whole gospel takes time, happening over a lifetime. It is with that conviction, born out of his own experience, that Geoff New offers us an honest, hopeful, articulation of how Jesus, the Great Preacher himself, shapes and molds us preachers for his glory. Walking us through the Lord's Prayer as seen in the life, death and resurrection of Jesus, Dr New takes us deep into the heart of Jesus, especially into Jesus's heart for those he calls to join him in his preaching. Oh how deep Dr New takes us! I wholeheartedly commend this powerful work of wisdom and grace!

Darrell Johnson
Retired Pastor and Professor
Teaching Fellow, Regent College, Vancouver, Canada

This is a fantastic and unique book: for starters, it is full of insights into all-too-familiar passages; more importantly, it guides us into a surprisingly deep and rich devotional life from the Scriptures. This is vital for preachers, for whom the Bible can degenerate into a mere "tool of the trade." Geoff New has provided us with some wonderful inspiration to sustain even the weariest of ministers.

Mark Meynell
Director, Europe and Caribbean, Langham Preaching

This practical and helpful book is essential reading for all who preach and teach. Geoff New draws on years of experience to lay a foundation for pastoral ministry and breathe new life into a familiar text. He takes us on a journey which illuminates the life, death and resurrection of Jesus. I was informed, challenged and inspired and have a new depth of appreciation for the Lord and his prayer.

This is a book you will want to keep on your desk, not your shelf, and you will recommend to others.

Nigel Pollock
President and CEO, InterVarsity Canada

Geoff New takes a new, inspiring look at the use of the Lord's Prayer by preachers and comes up with a deeper, insightful, challenging, and practical way of praying the Lord's Prayer. Like a master weaver, Geoff shows how preachers can use the Lord's Prayer as Christ did in his life, death and resurrection. Geoff challenges with insightful views and encourages preachers to pray. A must-read for all preachers of the word.

Frank Shayi
Principal Emeritus and Lecturer,
International College of Bible and Missions, Roodepoort, South Africa
Regional Coordinator, Southern Africa, Langham Preaching

We preachers regularly lead the congregation in praying the Lord's Prayer. In this fine book, Geoff New enables the Lord's Prayer to lead us. Fresh insights abound on every page. A wonderfully formative, inspiring, challenging book. Just what we preachers and pastors need.

Will Willimon
United Methodist Bishop, Retired
Professor of the Practice of Christian Ministry,
Duke University, Durham, North Carolina, USA

The Lord's Prayer in the Preacher's Life

Geoff New

© 2020 Geoff New

Published 2020 by Langham Preaching Resources
An imprint of Langham Publishing

www.langhampublishing.org

Langham Publishing and its imprints are a ministry of Langham Partnership

Langham Partnership
PO Box 296, Carlisle, Cumbria, CA3 9WZ, UK
www.langham.org

ISBNs:
978-1-78368-812-8 Print
978-1-78368-851-7 ePub
978-1-78368-853-1 PDF

Geoff New has asserted his right under the Copyright, Designs and Patents Act, 1988 to be identified as the Author of this work.

All rights reserved. No part of this publication may be reproduced, stored in a retrieval system or transmitted, in any form or by any means, electronic, mechanical, photocopying, recording or otherwise, without the prior written permission of the publisher or the Copyright Licensing Agency.

Requests to reuse content from Langham Publishing are processed through PLSclear. Please visit www.plsclear.com to complete your request.

Scriptures taken from the Holy Bible, New International Version®, NIV®. Copyright © 1973, 1978, 1984, 2011 by Biblica, Inc.™ Used by permission of Zondervan.

British Library Cataloguing-in-Publication Data
A catalogue record for this book is available from the British Library

ISBN: 978-1-78368-812-8

Cover & Book Design: projectluz.com

Langham Partnership actively supports theological dialogue and an author's right to publish but does not necessarily endorse the views and opinions set forth here or in works referenced within this publication, nor can we guarantee technical and grammatical correctness. Langham Partnership does not accept any responsibility or liability to persons or property as a consequence of the reading, use or interpretation of its published content.

For Paul – my preaching lecturer
You first taught me twenty-five years ago and have never stopped

Contents

Acknowledgements xi
Preface xiii
How to Use This Book xix
Introduction: The Lord's Prayer 1
Book Overview 11

Part I: The Lord's Prayer as Heard in Jesus's Life (Luke 18:1–19:10)

1 Our Father in Heaven 15
  A Prayer for Preachers Wanting to Pray

2 Hallowed Be Your Name 21
  A Prayer for Preachers Wanting to Honour God

3 Your Kingdom Come 27
  A Prayer for Preachers Wanting to Guide

4 Your Will Be Done on Earth as It Is in Heaven 33
  A Prayer for Preachers Wanting Renewal

5 Give Us Today Our Daily Bread 39
  A Prayer for Preachers Wanting Fulfilment

6 Forgive Us Our Debts as We Also Have Forgiven Our Debtors 45
  A Prayer for Preachers Wanting Understanding

7 Lead Us Not into Temptation 51
  A Prayer for Preachers Wanting Healing

8 Deliver Us from the Evil One 57
  A Prayer for Preachers Wanting Restoration

Part II: The Lord's Prayer as Heard in Jesus's Death (The Cries from the Cross)

9 Our Father in Heaven 65
  A Prayer for Preachers Needing Reassurance

10 Hallowed Be Your Name 71
  A Prayer for Preachers Needing Courage

11	Your Kingdom Come	77
	A Prayer for Preachers Needing Hope	
12	Your Will Be Done on Earth as It Is in Heaven	85
	A Prayer for Preachers Needing Family	
13	Give Us Today Our Daily Bread	91
	A Prayer for Preachers Needing Nourishment	
14	Forgive Us Our Debts as We Also Have Forgiven Our Debtors	97
	A Prayer for Preachers Needing Release	
15	Lead Us Not into Temptation	103
	A Prayer for Preachers Needing Enabling	
16	Deliver Us from the Evil One	109
	A Prayer for Preachers Needing Blessing	

Part III: The Lord's Prayer as Heard in Jesus's Resurrection (John 20:11–29; 21:1–23)

17	Our Father in Heaven	117
	A Prayer for Preachers Desiring Revelation	
18	Hallowed Be Your Name	123
	A Prayer for Preachers Desiring Faith	
19	Your Kingdom Come	129
	A Prayer for Preachers Desiring Peace	
20	Your Will Be Done on Earth as It Is in Heaven	135
	A Prayer for Preachers Desiring Direction	
21	Give Us Today Our Daily Bread	141
	A Prayer for Preachers Desiring Refreshment	
22	Forgive Us Our Debts as We Also Have Forgiven Our Debtors	147
	A Prayer for Preachers Desiring Kindness	
23	And Lead Us Not into Temptation	153
	A Prayer for Preachers Desiring Perseverance	
24	Deliver Us from the Evil One	159
	A Prayer for Preachers Desiring Vision	
Epilogue		165
Bibliography		167

Acknowledgements

This book has taken most of my lifetime to mature. In recent years there have been particular people who have been instrumental in seeing it written.

Rev Dr Paul Windsor (Director of Langham Preaching) whose faithful friendship has meant so much. This book would not have been written but for him. You continually offer me opportunity. Your skill, knowledge, counsel and direction have been the difference.

Rev Malcolm Gordon for saying the right things at the right time to set me right.

Rev Dr Martin Macaulay and East Taieri Presbyterian Church (New Zealand) who gifted me the opportunity to address their annual South Island Ministry Conference. It was my teaching there which gave me the vision for this book.

Rev Erin Pendreigh who spoke a timely, heart-felt and kind word which inspired me to do more with this material.

Rev Neil Thorogood (Principal) and the staff of Westminster College (Cambridge, UK) for their generosity in every way in providing space to begin my writing.

Rev Dr Steve Taylor (Principal) and my colleagues at the Knox Centre for Ministry and Leadership for helping me expand and test this material in our work.

Peter and Camilla Cathro, Marco and Maree Kleinlangevelsloo, Dr Esther "Bean" Dale, Nick and Rachel Bates – thank you for our meetings where we encounter green pastures, still waters and restoration of the soul with the Good Shepherd.

Josiah, Luke and Ali. Thank you for gifting the quality of life and fun that only family can give.

My daughter Rebekah who read draft chapters overnight and gifted me clarity and confidence.

Nathaniel, thank you for helping me type the manuscript and for your unbridled joy.

Ruth, my wife, who sees and hears me, but most importantly sees and hears God and teaches me in that.

Preface

On the morning of 4 November 2010, QANTAS flight QF32 left Singapore bound for Sydney, Australia. There were 440 passengers and 29 crew onboard. The aircraft, an Airbus A380, was one of the safest in the world. A few minutes after take-off one of the four engines exploded. There are twenty-two systems on an A380; twenty-one were either damaged or destroyed by the explosion. Warning signals and alarms blared in the cockpit and the onboard computer system produced over one hundred checklists for the crew to work through; a world record. Parts of the engine cover rained down on homes and businesses on the Indonesian island of Batam, with some landing on the roof of a school. One part had the QANTAS logo (a flying kangaroo) on it, resulting in news reports that the plane had crashed. For two hours the flight crew, under the leadership Captain Richard de Crespigny, kept the aircraft in the air while they assessed the damage before safely landing at Changi airport, Singapore. But for the skill of the pilot and his crew, this incident would have been one of the world's worst air disasters.

Using the flight number, Richard de Crespigny wrote a book about the experience simply entitled *QF32*. I was keen to read about the action of this mid-air drama. I began reading and was immediately drawn into the crisis. Four minutes after take-off the engine explodes. So far so good. The story was gripping and exciting. But then the story changed! The action stopped. The story went back in time to Crespigny's family and upbringing. In fact, the story went back centuries as Crespigny talked about the origins of his family name. I was disappointed. I wanted to read about the mid-air crisis, but now I was reading about his family tree and life growing up in Australia. But slowly I realized why this part of the story needed to be told; Crespigny's early life experiences had prepared him for the in-flight emergency of November 2010. This part of his story was about the experiences that formed him as a person and laid the foundations for a career as an accomplished pilot. One incident described in the book illustrates this powerfully.

As an eighteen-year-old, Crespigny joined the Royal Australian Air Force. On his first flight, the instructor commanded him to put the plane into a spin, causing it to lose altitude rapidly. Crespigny describes the terror of seeing farmland spiraling up towards him as they hurtled towards the ground in a plane out of control. He looked at the instructor in panic. The instructor simply looked back smiling with his arms crossed across his chest. He was not going to help. He winked and pointed back at Crespigny. The instructor was teaching this young, inexperienced pilot that he must respect the physical laws of gravity, speed and weight. His instructor was establishing a foundation in Crespigny's life. That day, Crespigny learned that no matter how advanced an aircraft is, the pilot still needs to fly it. Such life experiences were forming Crespigny for an unthinkable situation years later, on flight QF32, which resulted in him saving hundreds of lives.

As I read this, the pilot's story began to speak to me about the preacher's story. I thought about how God forms a preacher over a lifetime. I wondered about the early life experiences which shape the preacher's character and calling and find expression later, years later, through the sermons that are preached and the life that is lived for Christ. I wondered about the work of the Spirit preparing us so that, in the tradition of Esther, we are prepared for "such a time as this" (Esth 4:14). This book is about experiencing formation.

I was struck by the harsh lesson the pilot was taught as an eighteen-year-old to respect the physical forces encountered when flying. Gravity, speed and weight constantly test the pilot's skill. His instructor was establishing a foundation skill set in this young pilot. Again, the pilot's story began to speak to me about the preacher's story. What forces constantly test a preacher's skill? A preacher might have study aids or access to technology that can help in sermon preparation and delivery, but what foundational tasks does the preacher need to establish? This book is about establishing foundation.

The preacher's formation and the preacher's foundation: awareness and appreciation of both are necessary. In the ministry of preaching, preachers can be guilty of focusing only on the next sermon without considering who is preaching that sermon. Your sermon does not just reveal the Bible passage you are preaching from; it also reveals who is preaching it. You might not be revealed immediately or always – but you will be eventually. Preaching is a community event and the character and calling of the preacher will be experienced by the community through the sermon. Not immediately or always – but eventually. This is why consideration of your formation and foundation in Christ is so important as a preacher. None of the passengers on flight QF32 were aware of the captain's formation as a person or foundation as a pilot, but their lives were literally saved because of them. In the mid-air crisis, his formation and foundation mattered, and the truth of his life was experienced by hundreds of people on that aircraft. As a preacher you are charged with speaking the word of God, and it is a matter of eternal life and death. As a preacher your formation and foundation matter.

To be more precise about this, let us shift our attention from the story of a pilot to the story of a preacher. In 2 Timothy 1:3-14, the apostle Paul writes to the young preacher Timothy. Here in this passage Paul reminds Timothy of his formation and foundation. Read these words slowly:

> I thank God, whom I serve, as my ancestors did, with a clear conscience, as night and day I constantly remember you in my prayers. Recalling your tears, I long to see you, so that I may be filled with joy. I am reminded of your sincere faith, which first lived in your grandmother Lois and in your mother Eunice and, I am persuaded, now lives in you also.
>
> For this reason I remind you to fan into flame the gift of God, which is in you through the laying on of my hands. For the Spirit God gave us does not make us timid, but gives us power, love and self-discipline. So do not be ashamed of the testimony about our Lord or of me his prisoner. Rather, join with me in suffering for the gospel, by the power of God. He has saved us and called us to a holy life – not because of anything we have done but because of his own purpose and grace. This grace was given us in Christ Jesus before the beginning of time, but it has now been revealed through the appearing of our Savior, Christ Jesus, who has destroyed death and has brought life and immortality to light through the gospel. And of this gospel I was appointed a herald and an apostle and a teacher. That is why I am suffering as I am. Yet this is no cause for shame, because I know whom I have believed, and am convinced that he is able to guard what I have entrusted to him until that day.
>
> What you heard from me, keep as the pattern of sound teaching, with faith and love in Christ Jesus. Guard the good deposit that was entrusted to you – guard it with the help of the Holy Spirit who lives in us. (2 Tim 1:3-14)

Paul's encouragement to Timothy to continue to deepen his formation and foundation in Christ focuses on each aspect individually and blends the two. The themes of formation and foundation are two interwoven threads running through this portion of Scripture. Sometimes each thread is separate and sometimes they are wrapped around each other. Think of formation and foundation as identical twins. They are both very much alike, yet they each have their own personalities. With this in mind, and for the purpose of clarity, let's consider the distinct personalities of formation and foundation described in 1 Timothy 1:3–14.

Formation

Paul reminds Timothy (and us) to experience formation by fanning into flame the gift of God within us (2 Tim 1:6); through the Spirit of God who does not give fear but power, love and self-discipline (2 Tim 1:7); by suffering for the gospel (2 Tim 1:8, 12); by trusting the One we know (2 Tim 1:12); and by knowing that God guards what we entrust to him and that we, too, with the help of the Spirit, guard the good deposit given to us (2 Tim 1:12, 14). Such formation builds strong foundations in our life.

Your formation as a preacher matters.

Foundation

Paul reminds Timothy (and us) of the key people who established the foundations of our faith early in life (2 Tim 1:5); of the foundation of God's salvation, call and purpose (2 Tim 1:9); of the foundation of the grace of Christ Jesus given before the beginning of time (2 Tim 1:9); and the foundation of the pattern of sound teaching given by Paul (2 Tim 1:13). Such foundations nurture strong formation in our life.

Your foundation as a preacher matters.

But how might we attend to all that is within Paul's counsel to Timothy? How do we attend to the spiritual work necessary to grow in our character and call as preachers? We need a flight instructor. Such a person might be a Paul (2 Tim 1:13), a Lois or a Eunice (2 Tim 1:5). Whoever it is, we need someone who we can trust (2 Tim 1:12). Sometimes your life can be in a tailspin, and we need someone to show us how to use such experiences to learn to cope and enrich our ministry. We need someone to help us find God's message in seemingly irrelevant moments and experiences. We especially need someone to help us discern the presence of God in scary situations that are so dramatic we think only of the situation instead of where God is in it all.

Of course, such a person is Jesus Christ. One way Jesus attends to our formation and foundation is through the prayer of all prayers, the Lord's Prayer (Matt 6:9–13). Luke tells of the time the disciples watched Jesus pray and they asked, "Lord, teach us to pray" (Luke 11:1). This book makes the same request.

We will listen to Jesus pray the Lord's Prayer. Yet Jesus did not just say the words of the Lord's Prayer, he embodied it. We can observe the pattern of the Lord's Prayer in the pattern of Jesus's life, death and resurrection. The disciples in the gospels encountered the words and deeds of Jesus through his life, death and resurrection: we will seek to do the same through encountering the Lord's Prayer. Through a series of devotions on Jesus expressing the Lord's Prayer, we will experience formation in Jesus and establish our foundation as preachers.

And so this book is written in the prayerful hope that it will help you deepen and widen your character and call as a preacher. This book is written in the prayerful hope that your formation will expand and your foundation will strengthen.

Ephesians 3:20–21

Now to him who is able to do immeasurably more than all we ask or imagine, according to his power that is at work within us, to him be glory in the church and in Christ Jesus throughout all generations, for ever and ever! Amen.

How to Use This Book

The Lord's Prayer is familiar to us; maybe too familiar. As a result, we can miss its power and pray it without passion. You are invited to take a new and second look at this prayer. Much like the blind man who needed a second touch by Jesus (Mark 8:22–26): after the first touch he saw people looking like trees walking; after the second touch he could see. Or like Mary at the tomb (John 20:11–16). She, too, needed a second look. The first time she saw a gardener; the second time she realized it was the resurrected Christ.

This book will focus on the version of the Lord's Prayer as found in Matthew 6:9–13:

> This, then, is how you should pray:
>
> "Our Father in heaven,
> hallowed be your name,
> your kingdom come,
> your will be done,
>   on earth as it is in heaven.
> Give us today our daily bread.
> And forgive us our debts,
>   as we also have forgiven our debtors.
> And lead us not into temptation,
>   but deliver us from the evil one."

The prayer is found at the heart of Jesus's teaching known as the Sermon on the Mount (Matt 5–7).

The Introduction

The Introduction to this book will explain the nature of the Lord's Prayer and why its place in the Sermon on the Mount is so important. The Introduction is essential for you to read before continuing with other parts of the book.

The Parts

The rest of the book is arranged in three parts: (1) Jesus's life; (2) Jesus's death; (3) Jesus's resurrection. Each part will use gospel passages to illuminate and illustrate each phrase of the Lord's Prayer. Each part helps us hear the Lord's Prayer in new ways.

The gospel passages selected for Jesus's life (Luke 18:1–19:10), Jesus's death (the seven cries from the cross), and Jesus's resurrection (John 20:11–29; 21:1–23) represent the time immediately before his crucifixion, during his crucifixion and after his resurrection. So, while the Scriptures used range across the gospels, they are centred on a concentrated time period of Jesus's ministry.

Jesus's words and actions from these gospel passages help deepen our experience of the Lord's Prayer as preachers. Jesus's words and actions help us hear the Lord's Prayer in new ways. As we listen to the Lord's Prayer in Jesus's life, death and resurrection, it begins to echo in our lives and ministry as preachers.

The Chapters

After you have read the Introduction, you can read the chapters in any order. You will know the season you are in and what you need. You can read them as part of daily devotions (for individuals or groups) or simply take as needed by reading a chapter you think will be helpful.

Read Slowly and Aloud

Each chapter begins with a portion of Scripture. The portion of Scripture will be the focus for that chapter.

- Read the Scripture slowly and aloud.
- When we read Scripture slowly and aloud we are able to concentrate on the words better and are less likely to skip words than when we read silently. Indeed, you will find value in reading the portion of Scripture aloud two or three times before you continue with the rest of the chapter.
- When you have finished your reading of Scripture, be still in God's presence. Quiet your heart. Listen for God.

The Stories

Throughout this book you will notice that I draw on stories from my experiences as a preacher, pastor, and teacher of preaching.

Why?

Jesus once asked his disciples, "Who do people say I am?" (Mark 8:27). They gave him various answers about what people were saying. But then Jesus made the question very personal, "But what about you? Who do you say I am?" (Mark 8:29). When giving an answer about what others were saying, the disciples could do so at a safe distance. They were not committed to the answer. They could hide behind what others were saying. However, when Jesus asked them what *their* personal answer was, that was entirely different. What they said next would commit them. Their answer would reveal the nature of their relationship with Jesus. Jesus's question drew them closer and deeper.

The reason I draw on stories from my life is in response to the Scriptures used in this book. As I reflected on the Scriptures, I needed to respond. The Scriptures asked me, "But what about you?" They drew me closer and deeper. The stories I tell are my answers, and I hope they help draw you closer and deeper to the Scriptures. I offer these stories that you too may offer your stories in response to Jesus's question, "But what about you?" I offer my stories as an invitation for you to recall your stories in response to the Scriptures and the Lord's Prayer. As you do, may you experience the Author of Life writing more of his story in your life.

Introduction

The Lord's Prayer
Being Seen and Heard

Matthew 6:9–13

This, then, is how you should pray:

"Our Father in heaven,
hallowed be your name,
your kingdom come,
your will be done,
    on earth as it is in heaven.
Give us today our daily bread.
And forgive us our debts,
    as we also have forgiven our debtors.
And lead us not into temptation,
    but deliver us from the evil one."

Let's look at the place, power and purpose of the Lord's Prayer.

Do You See Me? Do You Hear Me?

In teaching the Lord's Prayer, Jesus places it in the context of how some people of his day observed three practices of the Jewish faith: giving, praying and fasting (Matt 6:1–8, 16–18). Some people of that time did these things to be heard and seen by others. They wanted their acts of righteousness to be heard by others, so when they gave to the poor, they announced it in the synagogues and on the streets. They wanted their acts of righteousness to be seen by others, so when they prayed, they stood in the synagogues and on street corners. When they fasted, they made it obvious by ensuring their face told the story. Jesus called them hypocrites and said they had already received their reward:

they had been seen and heard by others. They had been honoured by those who witnessed their supposed devotion to God. In giving these examples of spiritual practices, Jesus exposes human desires which are present within all of us to some degree:

1. I want to be seen
2. I want to be heard

From the most outgoing personality to the quietest personality, people harbour a need to know they are known.

Jesus's examples also show that in the attempt to be seen and heard, we are confronted by three questions:[1]

1. Who am I trying to impress?
2. What reward am I hoping for?
3. Who am I becoming?

The people Jesus describes in Matthew 6 are trying to impress other people, their reward is receiving people's admiration, and they have become hypocrites. Indeed, Jesus defines some of their prayers as being like that of pagans (Matt 6:7). So, what about us? We, too, have the desire, if not the need, to be seen and heard. The desire to be seen and heard is not a bad thing. Such desires reveal the human need to receive dignity, respect and the assurance that we belong to a community. These desires are not sinful in themselves but the way we seek to fulfil these desires can be. Jesus's examples illustrate the unhealthy ways some people seek to fulfil them.

Being Seen and Heard as a Preacher

As preachers we are on public display. Preaching requires that we are heard and seen. When we speak, it is in the hearing of a community of people. When we do something, it is in the sight of a community of people. In light of Jesus's descriptions of hypocrites in Matthew 6, the challenge is to examine who we are trying to impress, what reward we are hoping for and who we are becoming. The challenge is to engage in a ministry that is seen and heard but without becoming a hypocrite. As we ponder these challenges, Jesus provides a way to examine, explore and expand our lives: the Lord's Prayer (Matt 6:9–13). In contrast to the practice of the hypocrites of Matthew 6, Jesus counsels his

---

1. At the end of each chapter, there are questions for you to engage with. In addition to those questions, you might like to come back to these three questions from time to time.

disciples to go into their rooms, close their doors and pray to "your Father who is unseen" (Matt 6:6). Jesus calls his disciples to attend to acts of righteousness in secret: "Then your Father, who sees what is done in secret, will reward you" (Matt 6:4, 6, 18). Wrestling with the Lord's Prayer in your room with the door closed might be one of the most important spiritual practices you conduct as a preacher. Praying the Lord's Prayer is the best way to be seen and heard by the best person: our Father in heaven. The Lord's Prayer "*frees us* from a universal anxiety of the human heart. It frees us from the anxiety about whether or not we are praying in a way that pleases the Living God."[2] The Lord's Prayer assures us we are seen and heard by God.

A Familiar Prayer

The Lord's Prayer is very familiar to us. For some people, perhaps, this prayer has become too familiar and has lost its impact. When preparing to speak at a ministry conference, I decided to use the five one-hour teaching sessions to speak about the Lord's Prayer. Before the conference, I encountered people who questioned the wisdom of my topic choice. One person challenged me, "I would have thought the church knows about the Lord's Prayer. Why speak on that?" I replied, "That's the issue. We know it, we think we know, and yet we don't know it." He said, "Well, what are you going to say about it?" I paused. I had been working and wrestling with the Lord's Prayer for years by this stage. Lots of responses came to mind. I chose the one which had been dominating my thinking, "It's urgent." As a prayer, I have most often heard it prayed as if it is a house cat which meows. However, this is the prayer taught by the Lion of the Tribe of Judah, and it is meant to roar. This prayer is strong and demanding.

An Exodus Prayer

When the Gospel of Matthew records the Sermon on the Mount, Jesus ascends a mountain, sits down and teaches the people (Matt 5:1–2). This echoes Moses receiving the law on Mount Sinai and teaching Israel (Exod 19–23). Jesus is presented as a new Moses giving a new law and leading people on a new exodus. As Jesus teaches his new law, he teaches a new prayer to be at the heart of it: an exodus prayer. A prayer which calls on God to free us and the world from all that enslaves us. The importance of this prayer is evident in that it appears at the heart of the Sermon of the Mount (Matt 5–7). The Lord's Prayer

---

2. Johnson, *Fifty-Seven Words*, 13. Emphasis in original.

acts like a mirror at the very centre of the Sermon on the Mount. Everything Jesus said before the Lord's Prayer is mirrored after it. We can see how it works like this:

Jesus and the crowd (Matt 5:1–2)
    Those who are blessed (Matt 5:3–12)
        Being present/seen by the world & fulfilling the law/prophets (Matt 5:13–20)
            Living under the law of Christ (Matt 5:21–48)
                Giving and praying before God (Matt 6:1–6)
                    Danger of empty prayer (Matt 6:7–8)
                      The Lord's Prayer (Matt 6:9–13)
                    Danger of empty forgiveness (Matt 6:14–15)
                Fasting for God (Matt 6:16–18)
            Living under the rule of God (Matt 6:19–7:6)
        Summary of the law/prophets & being seen/heard by God (Matt 7:7–12)
    Those who are judged (Matt 7:13–27)
Jesus and the crowd (Matt 7:28–8:1)

The Lord's Prayer is the Sermon on the Mount in prayer form. The teaching and demands of the Sermon on the Mount are gathered up into this prayer of prayers. This prayer not only assures us we are seen and heard by God, it also guides us as we seek to impress our Father in heaven, look to him for our reward and become the kind of person he calls us to be.

An Urgent Prayer

One of the most common types of prayers we pray is called a petition.[3] A petition is the acknowledgement that we have constant need of God's work and word in our life. When we petition God, we are asking him for what we need. We are acknowledging we lack power and control over life, and we turn to God to act and speak. By petitioning God, we are saying, "Lord, we are in relationship with you." Petition is the kind of prayer we pray most naturally and often. Petition is the kind of prayer we pray when we are humbly aware that we are lesser and God is greater. Yet the words and phrases (the petitions) which make up the Lord's Prayer are surprisingly direct. The language is urgent

---

3. E.g. "Do not be anxious about anything, but in every situation, by prayer and petition, with thanksgiving, present your requests to God." Phil 4:6.

and bold. Each part of the prayer is more like a command than a petition or request.[4] In the time and culture in which Jesus taught this prayer, no one would speak to their superior in the direct way the Lord's Prayer is worded.[5] Yet Jesus invites us to pray to our Father in heaven by petitioning in precisely this way.

The first three petitions (hallowed be your name; your kingdom come; your will be done) are worded in a way whereby we reverently proclaim that which only God can do.[6] While this part of the prayer is command-like, it is not quite telling God what to do. The sense is more "Father, this needs to happen and only you can do it. So, Father, you honour your name; you bring your kingdom to come; you bring about your will on earth. We can't do it, but we need you to." The first three petitions are a mix of reverence, directness and dependence. This part of the prayer is praying, "Be done!"[7]

The second half of the prayer (give us; forgive us; lead us; deliver us) becomes more direct and bold. The prayer is energetic, passionate, intense and desperate. Consider this. The words of the Lord's Prayer are such that the petitions are commands; imperatives, grammatically speaking. They are demanding. So, for example, the last four petitions of the Lord's Prayer have the same force of language as when the disciples cried out in terror to Jesus in the storm (Matt 8:25), when Peter cried out to Jesus when he was sinking (Matt 14:30) and when the Canaanite woman pleaded with Jesus to drive the demon out of her daughter (Matt 15:22).[8] In other words, the Lord's Prayer is prayed with the same force as if you were crying out, "Lord, save us! We're going to drown!" (Matt 8:25), "Lord, save me!" (Matt 14:30) and "Lord, Son of David, have mercy on me! My daughter is demon-possessed and suffering terribly" (Matt 15:22). So, if the first part of the Lord's Prayer is saying, "Be done!," the second half is saying, "Do it!"[9]

The Petitions of the Lord's Prayer

We most often pray the Lord's Prayer as one prayer without pausing between parts. This is right and proper. However, the Lord's Prayer is made up of eight

---

4. Johnson, 19–21. The observations about the language and verbs in the Lord's Prayer appear in most Bible commentaries. Johnson summarises the scholarship on the Lord's Prayer simply and helpfully. I mainly draw on his work for this section of the chapter.
5. Johnson, 19–20.
6. Scaer, *Sermon on the Mount*, 162–163.
7. Johnson, *Fifty-Seven Words*, 21.
8. Scaer, *Sermon on the Mount*, 169.
9. Johnson, *Fifty-Seven Words*, 21.

parts. Each part is a prayer or petition in itself. Each petition is full of meaning and significance. Each petition says something about God and us. Each petition deepens our relationship with God and reveals his love towards us and this world. When praying the Lord's Prayer, if we slow down and concentrate on each petition, our experience and understanding of God is enriched. Life can be rushed and busy, and we pray at the same pace. To pray the Lord's prayer slowly with a spirit of stillness better leads to an experience and knowledge of God and his ways.

There is much that can be said about each of the eight petitions of the Lord's Prayer. However, at this point we will limit ourselves to one foundational observation for each petition. The rest of the book will examine each petition from a variety of angles.

Our Father in Heaven

The Gospel of Matthew was written first of all for Jewish believers. When Jesus said to pray "Our Father in heaven," those present at the Sermon on the Mount would have one thing in mind: Father of the exodus. That glorious part of Israel's history was the first time they encountered God as "Father" (Exod 4:22). As mentioned earlier in this chapter, the Gospel of Matthew presents Jesus as a new Moses giving a new law and leading people on a new exodus. As Jesus teaches his new law, he teaches a new prayer to be at the heart of it: an exodus prayer. "Our Father in heaven" is the Father of the exodus – the Father who frees us from that which enslaves us.

Hallowed Be Your Name

This petition reminds us of the commands such as having no gods before our Father in heaven, not making any idols, and not misusing God's name (Exod 20:3–7). Also, to know someone's name is to be in relationship with them and for them to reveal their character. To know someone's name is to have access to them. We pray "Hallowed be your name," honouring the Father's love towards us, enjoying access to him and seeking to live in accordance to the goodness of his character.

Your Kingdom Come

Here we pray that God's reign is increasingly present and visible in our world, and we look forward to the world to come. The delights and demands of the kingdom both comfort and challenge our place in the world. To pray this is to live as a citizen of the kingdom and act justly, love mercy and walk humbly with our God (Mic 6:8).

Your Will Be Done on Earth as It Is in Heaven

This petition gathers up the first three petitions by demanding and declaring that our Sovereign God brings his agenda to bear on the life of this world. In praying this petition, we are confronted with the unexpected ways by which God's will is expressed and the obedience and participation it requires of us.

Give Us Today Our Daily Bread

This prayer phrase means "give us tomorrow's blessing today." We are asking for a double blessing and our daily bread can refer to physical and spiritual needs. This petition calls on the extravagance of God's generosity. Biblical scholars point out that this is the only petition where the thing being asked for appears at the start of the sentence: it is literally, "The bread of us which we need (for tomorrow) give to us today."[10]

Forgive Us Our Debts, as We Also Have Forgiven Our Debtors

This is the only place in the New Testament where sin is connected with debt (as in a loan of money which is growing larger with interest). The idea is that God cancels the growing debt we owe him, and we bless others by cancelling their debt to us. The parable of the Unmerciful Servant (Matt 18:21–35) is one of the best illustrations of this petition.

Lead Us Not into Temptation

Here we are praying that our Father in heaven will keep us from falling. We are weak and at times find ourselves in – or place ourselves in – situations whereby we succumb to temptation (e.g. Prov 7; 1 Cor 10:13). This petition calls on God's faithfulness to keep us from our tendency as humans to be unfaithful.

Deliver Us from the Evil One

The prayer begins with "Our Father in heaven" and now ends by asking him to deliver us from the father of lies. We have an adversary, and he wants to

---

10. Scaer, *Sermon on the Mount*, 172.

steal, kill and destroy (John 10:10). All the previous seven petitions under the mighty hand of God disarm the evil one and lead to our deliverance and fullness of life (John 10:10).

If You Could Only Pray One Prayer

In one sermon, I said to the congregation, "I wonder what would happen if the Lord's Prayer was the only prayer we could pray?" I wondered aloud what if, for one hour, one week or one month, this was the only prayer we prayed? What if we only prayed the Lord's Prayer word for word, neither adding nor subtracting from Jesus's words? Would we consider the content of the Lord's Prayer enough to address those things we need to pray about? Or would we find it too limiting, and even think that it might restrict our relationship with Jesus? Perhaps there are other things we would want to talk about in prayer that we consider are not addressed in the Lord's Prayer. Yet the themes and issues that are covered in this short, deep, community prayer address all of life and faith. For example:

> **Adoption** – Our Father in heaven
> **Worship** – Hallowed be your name
> **Hope** – Your kingdom come
> **Surrender** – Your will be done on earth as it is in heaven
> **Provision** – Give us today our daily bread
> **Healing** – And forgive us our debts, as we also have forgiven our debtors
> **Faithfulness** – And lead us not into temptation
> **Protection** – But deliver us from the evil one

In the months after I preached that sermon, stories began to emerge. Unknown to me, a number of people who heard the sermon decided to take up the challenge: they experimented with praying using only the Lord's Prayer. Some planned to do it, while others found themselves in unexpected emergencies or difficulties, and in the shock of the moment, remembered the challenge. They told me that in their crisis they discovered the Lord's Prayer was the first and only prayer that came to their mind. They prayed it passionately using the prayer language gifted by Jesus. They reported stories of healing, peace and wisdom. Our Father in heaven heard them, saw them and answered them. The width, height, length and depth of the Lord's Prayer was sufficient.

The Lord's Prayer and the Life, Death and Resurrection of Jesus

We have considered the context of the Lord's Prayer and how Jesus used it to contrast the spiritual practices of those who sought to be seen and heard by others for their own self-image. We have seen how it reflects the exodus story and is a prayer for a new exodus. We have seen how the Lord's Prayer is at the heart of the Sermon on the Mount and summarizes it in prayer form. We have noted that the words and phrases of the prayer are urgent, strong and bold. We have glimpsed that if you could only ever pray one prayer, the Lord's Prayer is more than sufficient. With all this in mind, this book is an opportunity to respond to Jesus's invitation to "go into your room, close the door and pray to your Father, who is unseen. Then your Father, who sees what is done in secret, will reward you" (Matt 6:6). There you will be seen and heard by your Father in heaven. There you can examine your formation and foundation as a preacher. There you can consider the questions underlying our desire to be seen and heard: Who am I trying to impress? What reward am I hoping for? Who am I becoming?

For our purposes as preachers, this book is not simply an invitation to pray the Lord's Prayer; it is a challenge to prayerfully wrestle with it. To do this, we will reflect deeply on the Lord's Prayer by looking for evidence of it in Jesus's life, death and resurrection. We will listen for the Lord's Prayer in what Jesus said and did. As we examine Jesus's life, death and resurrection for signs of this prayer, may the spirit of Christ examine us: may we experience formation and foundation in Christ. May the Lord's Prayer echo ever stronger in our lives as preachers.

This book is arranged in three parts. In each part, chapter by chapter, the Lord's Prayer is studied phrase by phrase to demonstrate how the Lord's Prayer is heard in Jesus's words and actions. Each chapter focuses on one petition of the Lord's Prayer in the order we pray it. Each chapter reflects on a gospel passage that sounds a petition of the Lord's Prayer and in turn echoes it in your life as a preacher.

Part I: Chapters 1–8 The Lord's Prayer as Seen in Jesus's life (Luke 18:1–19:10)

In Luke 18:1–19:10, Jesus is drawing near to Jerusalem and his crucifixion. In part I, each petition of the Lord's Prayer is matched to Jesus's ministry in this section of Luke's gospel. Luke, the gospel writer, has not deliberately ordered this part of his gospel to match the Lord's Prayer. However, Jesus's actions and words in this portion of Scripture provide wondrous material for us to listen to the Lord's Prayer in Jesus's life.

In this part of the book, the order of the petitions of the Lord's Prayer will follow the order of the events in Luke 18:1–19:10.

Part II: Chapters 9–16 The Lord's Prayer as Seen in Jesus's Death (the Seven Cries from the Cross)

In part II, each petition of the Lord's Prayer is matched to one of the cries from the cross, and one petition is matched to the sign nailed to the cross. We will listen to the Lord's Prayer in his death.

For this part, the order of the Lord's Prayer is followed rather than the order of the cries from the cross.

Part III: Chapters 17–24 The Lord's Prayer as Seen in Jesus's Resurrection (John 20–21)

John's record of resurrection encounters provide material for us to listen to each petition of the Lord's Prayer.

For this part, the order of the Lord's Prayer is followed rather than the order of the events in John 20–21.

In listening to the Lord's Prayer in this way, we will discover that the Lord's Prayer is echoing in and from your life and ministry as a preacher. May you know that the Father sees and hears you and his desire is to reward you (Matt 6:6). May you continue to grow into the preacher God created you to be.

> Our Father in heaven,
> hallowed be your name,
> your kingdom come,
> your will be done,
> on earth as it is in heaven.
> Give us today our daily bread.
> And forgive us our debts,
> as we also have forgiven our debtors.
> And lead us not into temptation,
> but deliver us from the evil one.

Book Overview

The Lord's Prayer...	Part I ...as heard in Jesus's Life	Part II ...as heard in Jesus's Death	Part III ...as heard in Jesus's Resurrection
Our Father in heaven	Chapter 1 Luke 18:1–8 A prayer for preachers wanting to pray	Chapter 9 Mark 15:33–39 A prayer for preachers needing reassurance	Chapter 17 John 20:11–18 A prayer for preachers desiring revelation
Hallowed be your name	Chapter 2 Luke 18:9–14 A prayer for preachers wanting to honour God	Chapter 10 John 19:19–22 A prayer for preachers needing courage	Chapter 18 John 20:24–29 A prayer for preachers desiring faith
Your kingdom come	Chapter 3 Luke 18:15–17 A prayer for preachers wanting to guide	Chapter 11 Luke 23:35–43 A prayer for preachers needing hope	Chapter 19 John 20:19–20 A prayer for preachers desiring peace
Your will be done on earth as it is in heaven	Chapter 4 Luke 18:18–27 A prayer for preachers wanting renewal	Chapter 12 John 19:25–27 A prayer for preachers needing family	Chapter 20 John 20:21–23 A prayer for preachers desiring direction
Give us today our daily bread	Chapter 5 Luke 18:28–30 A prayer for preachers wanting fulfilment	Chapter 13 John 19:28–29 A prayer for preachers needing nourishment	Chapter 21 John 21:1–14 A prayer for preachers desiring refreshment
Forgive us our debts as we also have forgiven our debtors	Chapter 6 Luke 18:31–34 A prayer for preachers wanting understanding	Chapter 14 Luke 23:32–34 A prayer for preachers needing release	Chapter 22 John 21:15–17 A prayer for preachers desiring kindness
Lead us not into temptation	Chapter 7 Luke 18:35–43 A prayer for preachers wanting healing	Chapter 15 Luke 23:44–46 A prayer for preachers needing enabling	Chapter 23 John 21:18–19 A prayer for preachers desiring perseverance
But deliver us from the evil one	Chapter 8 Luke 19:1–10 A prayer for preachers wanting restoration	Chapter 16 John 19:30 A prayer for preachers needing blessing	Chapter 24 John 21:20–23 A prayer for preachers desiring vision

Part I

The Lord's Prayer as Heard in Jesus's Life

Luke 18:1–19:10

Part 1

The Lord's Prayer as Heard in Jesus' Life

Luke 1:1–18:30

1

Our Father in Heaven
A Prayer for Preachers Wanting to Pray

Luke 18:1–8

Then Jesus told his disciples a parable to show them that they should always pray and not give up. He said: "In a certain town there was a judge who neither feared God nor cared what people thought. And there was a widow in that town who kept coming to him with the plea, 'Grant me justice against my adversary.'

"For some time he refused. But finally he said to himself, 'Even though I don't fear God or care what people think, yet because this widow keeps bothering me, I will see that she gets justice, so that she won't eventually come and attack me!'"

And the Lord said, "Listen to what the unjust judge says. And will not God bring about justice for his chosen ones, who cry out to him day and night? Will he keep putting them off? I tell you, he will see that they get justice, and quickly. However, when the Son of Man comes, will he find faith on the earth?"

John 1:18 says, "No one has ever seen God, but the one and only Son, who is himself God and is in closest relationship with the Father, has made him known." In this parable Jesus makes known our Father in heaven in an unexpected way. He does so by telling a story which explores how we, in a world of injustice, might talk with our Father in heaven. Yet this world is not only marked with injustice; it is also one full of promise. Just before this story we read about the kingdom of God coming in its fullness and the coming of the Son of Man (Luke 17:20–37).

So the message in Luke 18:1–8 is to keep praying and to not lose heart. To help us see this, Jesus tells a David and Goliath type story.

In a certain town there was a weak and helpless person (a widow) who has to deal with a powerful godless person (an unjust judge). Actually, the widow has to deal with *two* Goliaths: the person who is her adversary and the judge who acts like an adversary.

Her situation is bleak.

She suffers injustice, and the one person who can grant her justice does not care about God or anyone else. The powerless widow needs help from the powerful judge because of a powerful adversary.

The problem for the widow is, at best, delay and, at worst, disregard.

What is she to do?

What would *you* do?

Jesus wants to know (Luke 18:8).

Our Father in heaven.

The purpose of his story is to inspire us to pray and not give up (Luke 18:1); but will we? When our prayers are met with delay or apparent disregard it is easy to give up. The danger is to fall into silence and surrender to powerful forces.

Yet the widow is our role model. Even though she represents the weak and vulnerable in society, she also represents mustard-seed faith. She does not give up, and finally the judge sees to it that she receives justice. But this judge is not a nice person. He is a picture of faithlessness towards God and others. It is hard to paint a more discouraging picture. The judge is very "I" centred. This is extraordinary. Here is someone who is divinely charged with administering justice among the people of God, yet he neither cares about the source of his authority nor the people he is meant to serve. Even the reasons for his decision finally to do his job are dishonourable. He just wants to be left alone and is concerned the widow will physically attack him. His words have the sense that he is afraid she will strike him (Luke 18:5). So, he grants her request. But this is not the startling part of the story. The startling part happens once the story has finished.

After telling this story, Jesus invites us to "listen to what the unjust judge says" (Luke 18:6). Given that this story is to inspire followers of Jesus to pray and not give up, surely we are meant to focus on the widow and not the judge.

No.

Jesus directs our attention to the unjust judge. As we focus on the power figure in the story, we reflect on our prayers to our Father in heaven. As we focus on an unpleasant power-figure (the unjust judge), we think about times in our prayer life when our Father in heaven delays, or so it seems. As we focus on the unjust judge, we wrestle with one of the major themes in the Gospel of Luke: the theme of delay.

It works like this. This parable of Jesus is a how-much-more story; the lesser pointing to the greater. If even a godless and uncaring judge (the lesser) grants justice, how much more will our Father in heaven (the greater) grant justice. If a widow persistently presents a request to an unjust judge and ultimately receives justice (by the lesser), how much more will your prayers be answered by our just and caring Father in heaven (by the greater). For those like the widow, who cry out day and night, Jesus says God will not be like the unjust judge and keep putting them off (Luke 18:7–8). Unlike the judge in the story, God will see that justice is served and will do so quickly. So, "listen to what the unjust judge says" (Luke 18:6), then consider how-much-more our Father in heaven will respond to those who cry out "day and night" (Luke 18:7).

Our Father in heaven.

If the widow could get an answer from someone like that, how much more will we receive an answer from Someone who is nothing like that?

But has this parable done its work in your life?

Jesus finishes the story with the challenging question, "However, when the Son of Man comes, will he find faith on the earth?" (Luke 18:8). This question is full of meaning. If our Father in heaven is nothing like the unjust judge, then how much more should we be like the widow.

"However, when the Son of Man comes, will he find faith on the earth?"

Jesus waits for an answer.

Think carefully before you answer. Be honest.

This parable is exposing how we talk to our Father in heaven. Actually, this parable is examining whether we will even continue to talk to our Father in heaven should justice be delayed in an unjust world. It examines us by using a rich biblical prayer tradition, "How long Lord?"

This short prayer is prayed frequently throughout the Bible. Indeed, the need to pray such a prayer can be traced to the Israelites in slavery in Egypt. In Exodus 2:23–25 we read:

> During that long period, the king of Egypt died. The Israelites groaned in their slavery and cried out, and their cry for help because of their slavery went up to God. God heard their groaning and he remembered his covenant with Abraham, with Isaac and with Jacob. So God looked on the Israelites and was concerned about them.

The Israelites in slavery and the widow are alike.

"How long Lord?" You will find this short prayer in many of the psalms, the prophets and even once in the book of Revelation. The prayer is the cry of someone who is experiencing injustice and pain in the world and a sense of delay from our Father in heaven.

"How long Lord?" The exact words of this prayer might not be in this parable but a strong echo of it is. This parable calls us to adopt such a prayer: "How long Lord?" But what does this short prayer reveal? The parable shows us that our prayers reveal what we think about God. A. W. Tozer wrote, "What comes into our minds when we think about God is the most important thing about us. . . . We tend by a secret law of the soul to move toward our mental image of God."[1]

Our Father in heaven.

What comes into your mind when you think about our Father in heaven? Especially when God seems to delay?

Your answer describes the image of our Father in heaven to which your soul cries out.

Your answer is found in the times when you have stopped praying and have given up.

Your answer is found in the prayers you pray as you prepare your sermon and before you preach.

Your answer is found in the thoughts you have when you deliver your sermon and you do not receive the response from people that you hoped for.

Your answer is found in the struggle you experience when you preach about the God who speaks and acts but seems silent and inactive in your life.

But is your answer in keeping with the God this parable points towards?

Our Father in heaven.

Our prayers reveal what we think about our Father in heaven. But the parable tells us something more: that they also reveal us. Our prayers reveal whether we are like the widow.

Years ago, I heard a sermon about Joseph languishing in prison after Pharaoh's cupbearer forgot him (Gen 40). Joseph had given him an accurate and favourable interpretation of his dream and asked the cupbearer to remember him. The cupbearer was released from prison and forgot Joseph. The preacher used that incident to highlight Joseph's character. He summed up the situation like this, "Delay reveals what is in the heart."

Joseph and the widow are alike.

The story of Job demonstrates the same thing. After thirty-seven chapters describing Job's tragedy and suffering, along with the mystery of God and his

---

1. Tozer, *Knowledge of the Holy*, 1.

ways, God finally speaks out of the storm (Job 38–41). God challenges the things he has heard Job and his friends say about God. In the time between their speech and God's response, their view of God was exposed. Then Job humbly declares that he spoke of things too wonderful for him and that, while he had heard of God, now he has seen God (Job 42:1–6).

Job and the widow are alike.

Our parable, with its prayerful "How long Lord?" message, does the same work. The presence of delay reveals much. Delay reveals what the person praying thinks of God's character and reveals his or her own character.

If the only teaching available about our Father in heaven was based on your prayer life; what would people learn?

The founding pastor of a church where I pastored had served there in the late 1950s and early 1960s. His name was Lewis and he was a gentle, thoughtful and much-loved pastor. By the time I became the pastor of the church, he was well on in years and living in retirement. One Sunday morning, just before worship, I received a phone call saying Lewis had died peacefully that morning. I talked for a while with the person who had phoned me with the news. We shared thoughts and memories about this beloved brother in Christ. However, the conversation ended in a way I did not expect. The person said, "You know, Lewis used to say, 'The congregation will always know if their pastor is praying.'" I immediately fell into silence. I had no words because at that time in my ministry I was not like the widow. I was prayerless. I had been for some time. An awkward silence descended on the phone conversation. The person on the other end of the phone had no idea why I had stopped speaking and why there was now silence. Finally, he broke the silence and said, "Oh well. I guess I had better go." The lesson of the parable of the Unjust Judge and the Persistent Widow was very present. That telephone conversation has remained very loud in my soul.

Our Father in heaven.

And Jesus still waits for an answer: "However, when the Son of Man comes, will he find faith on the earth?"

Will he find you have faith in "Our Father in heaven"?

Reflection

What three words describe you when God delays answering your prayers?

Pray

Our Father in heaven.

2

Hallowed Be Your Name
A Prayer for Preachers Wanting to Honour God

Luke 18:9–14

To some who were confident of their own righteousness and looked down on everyone else, Jesus told this parable: "Two men went up to the temple to pray, one a Pharisee and the other a tax collector. The Pharisee stood by himself and prayed: 'God, I thank you that I am not like other people – robbers, evildoers, adulterers – or even like this tax collector. I fast twice a week and give a tenth of all I get.'

"But the tax collector stood at a distance. He would not even look up to heaven, but beat his breast and said, 'God, have mercy on me, a sinner.'

"I tell you that this man, rather than the other, went home justified before God. For all those who exalt themselves will be humbled, and those who humble themselves will be exalted."

A warning: this parable is a trap. You will not escape it. And neither should you try. For in this parable, both characters pray standing alone (Luke 18:11, 13), meaning only God can hear what each is saying. But Jesus allows us to listen in on these two private prayers. As you listen to the two prayers, you will hear yourself. This is the inescapable power of the parable.

But take note of the reason for this parable, "To some who were confident of their own righteousness and looked down on everyone else, Jesus told this parable" (Luke 18:9). So this is not a parable primarily about how we pray to God. This is a parable about how we live before God and with others. This is not a parable about one part of our life. This is a parable about all of our life.

Hallowed be your name.

In wrestling with this parable, we have in mind that part of the Lord's Prayer which is our current focus: Hallowed be your name. It has been noted that for the Jew to pray "Hallowed be your name" meant they would have to be living it. The person praying "Hallowed be your name" could only honestly pray that if they were also honouring God's name in how they treated others. This parable tests if this is the case for us. At the heart of how we pray and act is the question, "Does this honour God's name?" We are ambassadors for Christ. How much more as preachers who pray? At the heart of how we pray and preach lies the answer to the questions, "Does my life honour God's name? Does my life say in word and deed, 'Hallowed be your name?'"

In the parable there is contrast after contrast as we listen to the two characters talk to God.

The Pharisee "stood by himself and prayed" (Luke 18:11), thinking he was near God. The tax collector "stood at a distance" (Luke 18:13), thinking he was far from God.

The Pharisee seems nothing but spiritual in the temple. His speech is described as what he "prayed" (Luke 18:11). The tax collector seems nothing but sinful in the temple. His speech is described as what he "said" (Luke 18:13).

The Pharisee prays looking at the tax collector (Luke 18:11). The tax collector prays unable to look at anyone (Luke 18:13).

The Pharisee prays about himself in relation to others (Luke 18:11–12). The tax collector prays for himself in relation to God (Luke 18:13).

The Pharisee prays based on who he is not (Luke 18:11). The tax collector prays based on who he is (Luke 18:13).

The Pharisee prays based on how he sees himself (Luke 18:11–12). The tax collector prays based on how God sees him (Luke 18:13).

The Pharisee prays unaware of the true heart of the tax collector (Luke 18:11). The tax collector prays aware of the true heart of God (Luke 18:13).

The Pharisee prays relying on his own greatness. The tax collector prays relying on God's greatness.

The Pharisee prays in a way that is hollow. The tax collector prays in a way that is holy.

Hallowed be your name.

Two people showing two kinds of spirituality. Only one can be said to be in keeping with "Hallowed be your name." Only one can be said to have prayed in a way that showed an understanding of God's name and character. Only one can be said to have prayed in a way that showed an understanding of who he was before God. John Stott wrote, "Humility is not another word for hypocrisy, pretending to be other than you are. Humility is another word for honesty, understanding who you are and how you have become what you are."[1] The tax collector shows such humility.

Call to mind the last prayer you prayed. If you can't remember the exact words you prayed, try to remember what you prayed about. Think about who or what was the focus of your prayer. You might have been alone or with others. You might have prayed in the silence of your heart or aloud.

Based on your last prayer, where would Jesus put you in this parable?

If we consider your prayer as a long version of "Hallowed be your name," who did you honour?

One of the spiritual truths this parable reveals is how we live is how we pray. Note the prayers of the Pharisee and the tax collector again. The spirit of their prayers was a commentary on their life. Whether they intended it to be or not. Their lives were full containers. Their prayer is what spilled out.

Hallowed be your name.

We preachers stand in a perilous place for our sermons have much in common with prayer. They are words about God, in the name of God and for God. And so they contain the same spiritual truth that this parable reveals about prayer. Not only are the nature of our lives found in what we pray but also in what we preach. How we live is how we pray. How we live is how we preach.

Our prayers and sermons are not the first indication as to whether we honour or dishonour God's name. That is established in how we live day-to-day long before we pray or preach. Our lives are full containers and our prayer and preaching is what spills out.

The purpose of this parable – to speak to those "who were confident of their own righteousness and looked down on everyone else" (Luke 18:9) – reaches into the preacher's practice. Our sermons will not always be windows into how we have been living our life. The sermon content will not always and every time be a commentary on how we have been living our life. But the spirit in which we preach will be. The way we prepare the sermon and the attitude in our heart at the time will always and every time be a commentary on our life. We can either preach like the Pharisee prayed, secretly condemning the hearts of those to whom we are preaching, or we can preach like the tax collector prayed, openly calling on the heart of God.

Hallowed be your name.

An early realization I had as a young pastor was that despite an outward appearance of success or confidence, people were often masking terrible

---

1. Stott, *Last Word*, 63.

tragedy and pain in their lives. People carry heavy burdens secretly. Another realization was that often people who asked complicated questions about God really only wanted to know, "Am I okay with God? Does he love me?" Their presence within the church was as those who could not even look up to heaven. Their heads were down, and they were quietly praying humble tax-collector prayers. But if you preach with the same kind of attitude as the Pharisee prayed, you will never see or hear such people in the way God does. Or as God wants you to. Instead, in exalting yourself you will be blind to the humble. You will be more concerned about your own righteousness and giftedness and will harbour a superior attitude.

Such a preaching ministry will be the kind that prompted the Scottish preacher, James Denney (1856–1917) to comment, "No man can give at once the impressions that he himself is clever and that Jesus Christ is mighty to save."[2] There is only room for one Messiah in the pulpit.

In this parable, where in the temple do you pray and preach from?

When you pray "Hallowed be your name," does the way you live your life make that prayer true or false?

I once visited a huge university chapel which was over five hundred years old. The chapel is very temple-like. Such is its magnificence that people are drawn to it, though most of those who attend worship are tourists. They come to experience the majesty of the building and the choir's beautiful singing. On the evening I was there, the chapel was full of hundreds of people. The worship service was formal and towards the end communion was celebrated. The minister invited all those wanting to receive the bread and cup to come forward. I waited for a long queue to form but very few people moved. So I made my way forward, surprised at how many people remained seated. As I walked down the aisle, I felt good about being able to respond to the minister's invitation. There was the sense of belonging to Jesus. I felt warmed by being able to take the bread and cup in remembrance of his death and promised return. I realized then that most, maybe all, of those who remained seated had done so because they were there for reasons other than worshipping Christ. Clearly most were tourists who were there to experience an event rather than worship.

When the service finished, the minister stood at the entrance of the chapel saying goodbye to people. As I passed him, I thought about how he had missed a wonderful opportunity. There had been Bible readings but no sermon. I thought that even a four-to-five-minute reflection on the Scriptures would have touched the multitude there. Most were there to see the sights and would never

---

2. James Denney, quoted in Stewart, *Heralds of God*, 74.

return. Why not take this opportunity?! My mind went to what I would do if I were the minister. My mind went to the small but effective changes I would make if I had such a regular opportunity in this place. My mind went to how lives could be rebuilt and a new song instilled in their hearts.

Of all the people in this story, who do you think went home justified before God (Luke 18:14)?

It wasn't until a few days later in church, listening to a sermon on the Lord's Prayer, that I realized it wasn't me! I don't even know what it was about the sermon that caused the scales to fall from my eyes. All I know is the work of the Lord's Prayer in that sermon exposed how confident of my own righteousness I had been and how I had looked down on everyone else (Luke 18:9). "At least I'm not like others who can't come up for communion. Or like this minister who fails to take the opportunity to preach the gospel." This embarrassing personal revelation was an answer to prayer. That week I had been praying only one phrase from the Lord's Prayer: Hallowed be your name. As mentioned at the start of this chapter, a Jew could pray "Hallowed be your name" only if they were truly living it. Here I was praying it but not living it. My prayer was in harmony with the Pharisee's (Luke 18:11–12) and out of tune with the tax collector's. My life was not honouring the name of God.

What about you? What do your prayers and preaching reveal about how your life honours God's name?

Hallowed be your name.

Reflection

Consider the content of your prayers and preaching. Do you sound more like the Pharisee or the tax collector? Why?

Pray

Hallowed be your name.

3

Your Kingdom Come
A Prayer for Preachers Wanting to Guide

Luke 18:15–17

People were also bringing babies to Jesus for him to place his hands on them. When the disciples saw this, they rebuked them. But Jesus called the children to him and said, "Let the little children come to me, and do not hinder them, for the kingdom of God belongs to such as these. Truly I tell you, anyone who will not receive the kingdom of God like a little child will never enter it."

In this story, the disciples stand in a position of power. They stand between the people with their children and Jesus. They observe what they think is an annoyance to Jesus and try to stop it. One biblical scholar explains that, given how children were viewed at that time, the disciples' attitude is "easily understood, even justifiable."[1] Overall, children were considered as "not-adults" and so were not honoured or treated with any sense of importance.[2] The disciples were influenced by the culture they lived in. Children often died young from sickness, were killed or abandoned. If they had any value, it would mainly be if they could help the family generate income in the present or future, especially if they worked the land. The disciples had this mindset about children. They considered Jesus to have more important people to see. Jesus, however, had a different mindset.

Your kingdom come.

The disciples failed to recognize they were hindering citizens of the kingdom of God. The disciples were acting like guards at the gates of the

---

1. Green, *Gospel of Luke*, 651.
2. Green, 650–651.

kingdom. They were deciding who was allowed access to the king and rebuking people trying to bring babies to him. Jesus gives a strong challenge to the disciples. Jesus's message of "come to me" contrasts with his disciples' message of "stay away." Jesus contrasts the disciples' guard-like attitude with the children's guide-like example. The nature of little children is an example of how to receive and enter the kingdom. Jesus's message to the disciples is to stop being a guard who hinders people from entering the kingdom but become a guide who helps people enter the kingdom. Consider the children and learn.

Your kingdom come.

The events in Luke 18:15–17 challenge us to nurture a child-like attitude in spiritual matters. Preachers need to be guides who help people receive the kingdom rather than guards who hinder them. This incident in Luke 18:15–17 humbles us as preachers. The story is centred on babies and little children and reflects a consistent scriptural truth: the biblical story turns on the birth of babies. Time and again, the Scriptures take time to relate the circumstances around the birth of a child and how that leads to redemption for the people of God. We see it in the birth narratives and stories of children such as Isaac (Gen 21:1–6), Moses (Exod 2:1–10), Samson (Judg 13:1–25), Obed, the grandfather of David (Ruth 4:13–17), Samuel (1 Sam 1:1–20; 3:1–21), John the Baptist (Luke 1:5–25, 57–66) and, of course, Jesus (Matt 1:18–25; Luke 1:26–38; 2:1–7, 41–52). The ways of God are seen in the stories of the vulnerable as much as they are in the stories of the strong.

Your kingdom come.

As preachers, we can stand in a similar position as the disciples in this story. By the nature of our ministry, we are in a position of power. That position is one whereby we preach about God and his kingdom. People who listen to our sermons trust we know what we are talking about. They expect our sermons are based on good study and training. Therefore, people tend to place more significance and importance on what we say than they might for those who are not preachers. Yet, we may not realize the potential danger in this. People can consider us to be more spiritual than we really are. They can think that as preachers we are closer to God than they are. They can be overawed by us. During a worship service, I interviewed several people about their experience of fear. For example, one person had a fear of being in a small space which made travelling in planes a problem. Her husband was a pilot. Someone else was afraid of being in large areas with lots of people. We talked about how they coped with their fears through their faith in Christ. When the worship service finished, someone came up to me and said, "I have a fear." I replied, "Oh really? What is your fear?" She answered, "You!" I was shocked. It also seemed that she did not mean to be so honest. She gasped. She put her hand over her mouth and rushed off. This encounter gave me a lot to think about as a preacher: what was it about me and my ministry that caused someone to be afraid? Was I more like a kingdom guard than a kingdom guide?

So, the picture of Luke 18:15–17 is a suitable one to reflect on the quality that marks our preaching. Like the disciples in Luke 18:15–17, we are faced with people wanting to get closer to Jesus. The issue is whether we preach like a kingdom guard or a kingdom guide. The quality of our preaching can either be like a rebuke which hinders people approaching Jesus or like little children who help model how this kingdom is received. When speaking of the kingdom, our preaching can be conformed to our culture or informed by Christ. To be conformed by our culture can mean we value some people and devalue others, but this is in conflict with the kingdom of God. To be informed by Christ means that we consider all to be worthy of dignity because they are children of our Father in heaven. Whatever else we might preach, when we preach about receiving the kingdom of God, Jesus calls us to remember that it is child-like in its simplicity and as delightful as child's play. We are called to remember that a child exhibits a trusting reliance and dependence on their parents. Such a trusting and dependent faith is a necessary requirement for those who want to enter the kingdom. As preachers, it helps if we watch out for examples of child-like faith. Such examples teach us about the kingdom. Such examples help us as preachers and change how we see the world. We become less like guards and more like guides.

At the time of writing this, my grandson is eighteen months old. He can only say a few words, but he is still able to communicate through other means. One thing he regularly does is take me by the hand and guide me to something of great interest to him. Often when we get to what he wants to show me, he will pull on my hand so that I will sit on the floor or ground with him. He brings me to his level and then I am better able to see what he sees, to experience what he experiences. What might appear to be ordinary to an adult is a source of great delight to this small child. A leaf on the ground holds as much delight as seeing an elephant. A toy becomes the means to play a game of let's-pretend. A book is read not word-by-word in order but by pointing to colours and pictures, with pages read out of order and some words read and many missed out. The book is read in such a way that a never before-told story is shared between the two of us. He takes me to small spaces behind furniture. Places I would not normally crawl into as an adult. He changes how I speak, what I see and how I feel. He shows me the world through the eyes of a child and helps me experience the world with new delight. He changes my guard-like attitude with his guide-like example.

Your kingdom come.

To pray "Your kingdom come" might result in the quality of our preaching being impacted by examples of child-like qualities. "Your kingdom come" might be answered by examples which cause us to re-examine our values and behaviours. Let me give you two further examples of when I was unexpectedly challenged by two very different child-like encounters. Both have stayed with me and affected me as a preacher.

In the church I was pastoring, there was a special member of the church. For the purposes of telling this story, I will refer to her as Mary (though that is not her real name). Mary was an adult but had intellectual limitations which meant she was child-like. Mary could be very talkative and sometimes it proved difficult to finish a conversation with her. In this church, it was our practice during worship services to give people an opportunity to stand at the front and briefly talk to the congregation. Sometimes the invitation was to speak about any aspect of their faith and sometimes a topic was suggested. Whenever I made the invitation during a worship service, I never knew who would respond. One day I gave an invitation and for the first time Mary walked to the front of the church. As she approached, I became worried as I thought Mary would talk too long and it would be awkward having to interrupt her in front of everyone. Mary then turned to face the congregation. I could not believe what happened next; it was as if all her limitations disappeared. She spoke about one of the members of the church whose mother was dying. Mary called the church to pray for this family. I was astonished. I was the pastor and I was unaware of what this family was dealing with, yet Mary knew all about it. Furthermore, she was now leading the church in prayer. Then she returned to her seat. The congregation was very quiet. Something holy had just taken place. Thereafter, Mary regularly would come up to the front and speak to the congregation. She would have the people roaring in laughter or, other times, listening very carefully. People loved it when Mary contributed and guided us. There was beauty about it. But best of all she was showing us how to receive the kingdom of God. She did it so well, just like a little child would.

Your kingdom come.

During World War 2, the city of Stuttgart in Germany was bombed from the air over fifty times. Nearly half of the city was destroyed, and 4500 citizens died. After the war, the ruins of the buildings were piled on top of a hill called Birkenkopf, raising it by another forty metres. Birkenkopf is known by the residents of Stuttgart as Monte Scherbelino, which means Mount Shards. Today, there is a huge cross on top of the hill and during summer there are weekly Sunday worship services held there.

My wife and I visited Birkenkopf once. We were with a German friend and as we approached the hill, our friend asked a young father with his small boy for directions. They too were going to Birkenkopf. After a brief conversation in German, the father and boy walked on ahead of us. The boy yelled back to our friend in German. Our friend explained, "He just said, 'We are off to walk on the dead.'" She commented that his father had obviously tried to explain what the hill represented, and in true child-like fashion, he interpreted it plainly and simply, even if very bluntly. In a jarring way, this child had rightly declared the truth of this place. We were not simply visiting a hill made of broken buildings; we were about to visit a hill of broken people. He was guiding us. We were about to visit a graveyard.

So, we walked up the hill, and as we turned a corner, suddenly there it was! The first pile of ruins from a destroyed city. I am not sure what I expected, but my heart skipped a beat. I stopped and took in the sight. The view was confronting and overwhelming. But as I stood there, a group of four young women gathered at the bottom of the pile of ruins. Three of them climbed onto the stones and began to pose like fashion models while the fourth took photos. A bottle of wine was at the photographer's feet waiting to be opened. The ruins were confronting and so were the young women's actions. The words of the small child spoken shortly before, "We are off to walk on the dead," took on a prophetic edge as I watched the group of friends posing on the graves of unknown victims. For there, at the base of the rubble where the group of friends were having fun, was a sign in German which, when translated, reads, "This mountain built from the ruins of the city, after World War 2, stands here in remembrance of the victims and as a warning for the living."

The child showed more awareness and respect for this message than people years older than him who were following the culture of their time. People who lay, sat and posed on stones without even noticing the invitation to remember and the warning to heed.

Your kingdom come.

May you preach as a kingdom guide inspired by the qualities of little children.

Reflection

Call to mind a time when a child said or did something which was beautifully and naturally child-like. What spiritual lesson is God teaching you through that?

Pray

Your kingdom come.

4

Your Will Be Done on Earth as It Is in Heaven
A Prayer for Preachers Wanting Renewal

Luke 18:18–27

> A certain ruler asked him, "Good teacher, what must I do to inherit eternal life?"
>
> "Why do you call me good?" Jesus answered. "No one is good – except God alone. You know the commandments: 'You shall not commit adultery, you shall not murder, you shall not steal, you shall not give false testimony, honor your father and mother.'"
>
> "All these I have kept since I was a boy," he said.
>
> When Jesus heard this, he said to him, "You still lack one thing. Sell everything you have and give to the poor, and you will have treasure in heaven. Then come, follow me."
>
> When he heard this, he became very sad, because he was very wealthy. Jesus looked at him and said, "How hard it is for the rich to enter the kingdom of God! Indeed, it is easier for a camel to go through the eye of a needle than for somcone who is rich to enter the kingdom of God."
>
> Those who heard this asked, "Who then can be saved?"
>
> Jesus replied, "What is impossible with human beings is possible with God."

This story has power. As we read it, the story causes us to move from looking at the story, to then looking at ourselves, and then to looking at God. Overall, it causes us to reflect on, "Your will be done on earth as it is in heaven."

When we first look at the story, we do so from a safe distance. The characters and situation are vastly different from our own experience. For example, we are not a wealthy Jewish ruler. So, we look at the story in a way as more entertainment than engagement. We see a person of influence in a confronting conversation with Jesus. The action happens to someone else and not to us. We watch from a safe distance. The story has entertainment value.

The rich ruler starts with a question which is heavy with meaning. He addresses Jesus as "good," to which Jesus responds by saying only God is good. Rabbis taught that goodness was something only God possessed and so no one would usually say what the rich ruler had said. While we know that Jesus did possess goodness, the rich ruler shows he is not really thinking carefully about his words.[1] Jesus's response reveals that. As the conversation unfolds it becomes obvious that the rich ruler is not thinking carefully about his life either.

The key thing the rich ruler wants to know is "What must I do to inherit eternal life?" (Luke 18:18). In Jewish thought, life is about observance of the commandments and living justly. This was a commitment to act justly, love mercy and walk humbly with God (Mic 6:8). The immediate concern was about faithful earthly life; concern over eternal life followed after.[2] Jesus answers the question by providing a summary of the Ten Commandments (Exod 20:1–17). Yet, Jesus only names five of the commandments. To the rich ruler such an answer from a rabbi would seem normal. Rabbis would summarize the law to talk about the overall message of the law. The rich ruler is pleased: in his opinion he has kept all the commandments since he was a boy. If the rich ruler prayed "Your will be done, on earth as it is in heaven," he would be confident it was fulfilled in his life.

However, Jesus quoting some of the Ten Commandments is not simply a summary; it is a search. In the Ten Commandments, four commandments relate to loving the Lord your God (Exod 20:2–7). Jesus quotes none of them. The remaining six commandments relate to loving your neighbour. Jesus quotes five of them. The missing one is "Do not covet" (Exod 20:17). Jesus is exploring the rich ruler's life. Who or what is his god? Jesus's summary of the Ten Commandments reveals that wealth is the rich ruler's god.

When the rich ruler says he has kept the commandments, Jesus does not list the missing ones. He summarizes again, "You still lack one thing" (Luke 18:22). Jesus then confronts the idol in the rich ruler's life: "Sell everything you have and give to the poor, and you will have treasure in heaven. Then

---
1. Morris, *Luke*, 266–268.
2. Robinson, *Essential Judaism*, 193.

come, follow me" (Luke 18:22). When the rich ruler hears this, a great sadness descends on him. His wealth was too great and his devotion to his idol too strong. Jesus emphasizes the hold this god has on the rich ruler: "How hard it is for the rich to enter the kingdom of God!" (Luke 18:24). The lack of observing one of the love-your-neighbour commandments has a profound effect on the love-the-Lord-your-God commandments.

Your will be done on earth as it is in heaven.

Those present there that day are shocked. If the rich cannot enter the kingdom of God, who can?! For wealth was considered a sign of God's blessing. But Jesus has discerned a lack in the rich ruler's life which hindered him from following Jesus. One author describes the challenge well: "The problem is not that we've tried faith and found it wanting, but that we've tried mammon [money] and found it addictive, and as a result find following Christ inconvenient."[3] This raises an important spiritual challenge for us: what has a hold on us?

So, we move from looking at the story to looking at ourselves.

Imagine you were in the crowd when the rich ruler approached Jesus and the conversation turned to you. Imagine Jesus took the same approach and summarized the Ten Commandments and said to you, "You still lack one thing." Which commandment would be missing? Of the Ten Commandments, which love-your-neighbour commandment would be missing that exposes your hinderance in pursuing the love-the-Lord-your-God commandments?

Your will be done on earth as it is in heaven.

All Ten Commandments are repeated and applied in different parts of the New Testament.[4] The New Testament texts provide a helpful lens for us to explore whether we "still lack one thing." Consider these New Testament re-statements of the love-your-neighbour commandments to reflect on your life in Christ:

- Do you treat your parents honourably? (Eph 6:1–3)
- Do you harbour anger or hate, which Scripture likens to murder, against a brother or sister? (Matt 5:21–26; 1 John 3:11–15)
- Do you entertain adulterous thoughts in your heart? (Matt 5:27–30; Rom 13:9)
- Do you steal? (Rom 13:9; Eph 4:28)
- Do you lie? (Matt 5:33–37; Eph 4:25; 1 John 4:20)

---

3. Simon, *How Much Is Enough?*, 21.
4. Fee and Stuart, *How to Read the Bible*, 174–175.

- Do you covet other people's possessions and wealth and are you consumed by greed? (Rom 13:9; Eph 5:3; Jas 4:2)

Which one of these might have such a hold on your life that it has become your god? You stand and preach God but is he the God of your life? None of this is comfortable to reflect on, yet as those who preach the Scriptures, it is necessary. In Luke 18:18–27, the rich ruler was someone who others viewed as representing evidence of God's favour. But Jesus challenged that and searched the rich ruler's life to reveal his deep lack. As preachers, we too can be viewed by others as those who represent God's favour. We preach the word of God and speak in his name. People can credit us with spiritual depth, yet God alone knows how truly deep it is. So, the rich ruler is our representative. His question and response open us up to the same kind of conversation with Jesus. Hold your place in this gospel story. Stand before Jesus and ask him if you "still lack one thing."

In one of the countries I visit to conduct preaching training, foreigners are not allowed to bring any local currency into the country. You have to obtain cash once you are there. This means there is no point taking local cash with you when you leave the country to go home. You cannot bring it back when you return. Every time I am in this country and my time to return home draws near, my mind goes to what it must be like to die. I am unable to put the money to any future use in the place where I am going. So, at the end of every trip, I delight in trying to get rid of my money. I give some away and I spend some of it. However, I ensure I have a little left in case I unexpectedly need it at the airport just before I leave.

On one trip I was at the airport to leave for home. As soon as I arrived inside the airport, an official looking man immediately helped me with my bags and guided me to the airline counter. I thought he worked for the airline. After I had checked in, the man stood there and held out his hand. It was then I realized he did not work for the airline and that he looked for foreigners to help. He now wanted payment. Here was an opportunity to ensure I was not left with money I could not use. But I have to confess that I was annoyed as I felt I had been tricked. I handed him some money but the amount was tiny. I had more money I could have given. Now we were both annoyed. I was annoyed at having to give him money, and he was annoyed at what he had received. We parted ways. I was later confronted by the revelation that the small amount of money I gave matched the smallness of my heart. I was ashamed at my annoyed reaction. I was shocked at how much value I was putting on such a small amount. I am sure Jesus would have said to me that day, "You still lack one thing."

Your will be done on earth as it is in heaven.

There might be fear in this prayer being answered in your life. You might be afraid of giving something up because it threatens to create a huge lack in your life. You have become used to a way of living, even if it is at odds with the gospel. You cannot imagine life without that which you are being challenged to surrender. The thought of losing it causes great sadness for you. You might even think your future as a preacher is threatened. The rich ruler saw that his future was threatened. Jesus had told him he lacked one thing and then asked him to create an enormous lack: to sell all he had and give to the poor. Discovering which love-your-neighbour commandment is lacking in our life reveals which area we do not want God to have control over. That is a challenging discovery to make.

So, we move from looking at the story, to looking at ourselves, to looking at God.

The rich ruler was saddened. He only saw what he was losing, not what he was gaining. Jesus promised if he did what was being asked of him then, "You will have treasure in heaven. Then come, follow me" (Luke 18:22). Here was a clear connection with "Your will be done on earth as it is in heaven." But the rich ruler could not say yes to Jesus. The witnesses to the encounter between the rich ruler and Jesus were dismayed. "Who then can be saved?" (Luke 18:26). Possibly, you share that dismay as you stare at the idol in your life, unsure if you are able to part with it. But the gospel shows us that God creates a lack in our life to bring fullness. This story is a wonderful example of that. This story illustrates Jesus's words, "For whoever wants to save their life will lose it, but whoever loses their life for me will save it." (Luke 9:24). The rich ruler was an example of gaining the world but losing his very self (Luke 9:23–26).

Your will be done on earth as it is in heaven.

Do not dismay. "Jesus replied, 'What is impossible with human beings is possible with God'" (Luke 18:27). In Romans 7, Paul reflects on his inner battle in trying to do the right thing before God but failing. He is confronted with the impossibility of conquering his sinful impulses by relying on human effort. His honest and raw reflection is not out of place with the story here in Luke 18. Neither is his reflection on the difference God makes through the work of Jesus as we respond to Jesus's call to follow him: "What a wretched man I am! Who will rescue me from this body that is subject to death? Thanks be to God, who delivers me through Jesus Christ our Lord!" (Rom 7:24–25).

Your will be done on earth as it is in heaven.

Reflection

"You still lack one thing." Imagine Jesus directing these words to you. Which one of the Ten Commandments exposes a lack in your life?

Pray

Your will be done on earth as it is in heaven.

5

Give Us Today Our Daily Bread
A Prayer for Preachers Wanting Fulfilment

Luke 18:28–30

Peter said to him, "We have left all we had to follow you!"
"Truly I tell you," Jesus said to them, "no one who has left home or wife or brothers or sisters or parents or children for the sake of the kingdom of God will fail to receive many times as much in this age, and in the age to come eternal life."

In the movie *Even Money* (2006), the story is told about three people who destroy their lives because of addiction to gambling. The movie begins with one of the main characters saying:

> If you want to find the truth about someone, find their dream and work backwards. We're all chasing something. More money, more love. I don't know – maybe just one more chance. What we're really looking for is more life. Yes sir – more of this beautiful life. But if you're not careful you might go looking for more and wind up with less.

These words contain a disturbing warning about how life can be lived. We can pursue life in destructive ways only to discover that we have found death not life. We can invest our energy into what we think will satisfy only to discover that we are empty and famished.

Give us today our daily bread.

Peter's words to Jesus seem to have this worry at the heart of them. When Peter says, "We have left all we had to follow you!" (Luke 18:28), he is basically asking, "Is it worth it? Have we found life?" Peter is asking because Jesus has just spoken to the rich ruler (Luke 18:18–27). Jesus challenged the ruler to sell all and follow him. The ruler became very sad because he was very rich. This prompted Jesus to say how hard it is for the rich to enter the kingdom of God. Jesus words were shocking. During the time Jesus lived, riches were considered a blessing of God. So, if a rich ruler could not enter the kingdom, what chance did anyone have? Having witnessed this conversation, Peter checks with Jesus about his and the other disciples' status concerning the kingdom. "We have left all we had to follow you! Do we have life? Is what we are pursuing worth it?" Behind the question is the need to know, "What is my reward for following you?" Jesus has just redefined the place of wealth in a disciple's life – so now what? In Peter's words there is the idea of God being in our debt.

Give us today our daily bread.

Peter's question is on our behalf, not just on behalf of the disciples there that day. Within our hearts is a hunger. That hunger is for assurance that God recognizes our service to him and his mission. To a greater or lesser degree, we hunger for signs that what we do for God results in some kind of reward and recognition. By reward and recognition, I am not referring to the desire for encouragement and positive feedback after we have preached. That is normal and right. We are human and need to know if our preaching helps others and where we can improve. So, I am not referring to that kind of reward and recognition.

The kind of hunger I am referring to is the dangerous kind. The kind which slowly changes our heart, so we think that God owes us. This hunger has us seeking reward and recognition in ways which draw us away from the life of God. An example is the older brother in the parable of the Prodigal Son (Luke 15:11–32). When he sees that his repentant younger brother is welcomed home, the older brother complains bitterly to his father: "Look! All these years I've been slaving for you and never disobeyed your orders. Yet you never gave me even a young goat so I could celebrate with my friends. But when this son of yours who has squandered your property with prostitutes comes home, you kill the fattened calf for him!" (Luke 15:29–30).

The danger is such anger can be in our heart without realizing it. Such anger grows when we think we are not receiving from God what we deserve. Often, not always, such an expectation is centred on wealth and material goods.

A question to test ourselves is "How much money would it take for me to stop preaching?" Before you dismiss the question as not applying to you, consider the temptations of Jesus (Luke 4:1–13). Satan offered Jesus things and opportunities which would have met different kinds of hungers but all at the expense of Jesus forsaking his Father and mission. Two of the three temptations related to physical needs and wealth.

One day, a married couple in the church I pastored asked to come and see me. The request seemed urgent, so I thought it was some kind of emergency. But when they arrived, they began to talk to me and my wife about a get-rich scheme they wanted us to join. They showed us a beautiful coloured booklet with stories of people who now had so much money they no longer needed to work. They highlighted one story in particular. The person had been a pastor, but as a result of joining the scheme, he no longer needed to be in ministry. He and his wife now had enough money to be on holiday all the time. I explained to them that showing me such a story had entirely the opposite effect to what they were hoping for.

In Genesis 3, the serpent's lie to Adam and Eve was that God was misleading them. The lie was that God could be giving them more than they were receiving. That lie still has the potential to cause us to demand rewards and recognition from God:

> A great illusion is abroad in the land (whispered, I am told, by some serpent) that God is a wet blanket [someone who spoils fun] and that if we follow God, we will be cheated of the pleasure we are entitled to, robbed of fulfilment and happiness. A companion illusion is that if we do what we feel like doing, we will be blessed. The drink is intoxicating. But it is pure poison.[1]

"We have left all we had to follow you!" I wonder what you expect from God as a result of the sacrifices you have made as a preacher.

The apostle Paul provides a helpful case-study of someone who left all to follow Jesus. When Paul was chained in a prison, he wrote to the church in Philippi. He wrote about the nature of his reward and recognition: "But whatever were gains to me I now consider loss for the sake of Christ. What is more, I consider everything a loss because of the surpassing worth of knowing Christ Jesus my Lord, for whose sake I have lost all things. I consider them garbage, that I may gain Christ and be found in him" (Phil 3:7–9). Paul continues to describe his experience of Jesus. His measure of God's reward and recognition is according to the presence of Christ rather than material wealth: "I know what it is to be in need, and I know what it is to have plenty. I have learned the secret of being content in any and every situation, whether well fed or hungry, whether living in plenty or in want. I can do all this through him who gives me strength" (Phil 4:12–13).

---

1. Simon, *How Much Is Enough?*, 81.

Paul's words give us a vision of what Jesus described in response to Peter's cry. Jesus promised Peter that anyone who left loved ones or things they loved would "receive many more times as much in this age, and in the age to come eternal life" (Luke 18:29–30).

Throughout history, we have examples of people who have understood this and provided helpful insights for us. In the 1500s, one church leader wrote:

> We should not fix our desires on health or sickness, wealth or poverty, success or failure, a long life or a short one. For everything has the potential of calling forth in us a more loving response to our life forever with God.
>
> Our only desire and our one choice should be this: I want, and I choose what better leads to God's deepening life in me.[2]

Now that is a beautiful reward: "God's deepening life in me." This insight invites us to see beyond the variety of aspects by which we might measure quality of life (e.g. wealth, health, success, etc.) and instead discern the life of God in all circumstances. The ultimate measure of our reward and recognition is the life of God in us. Rabbi Abraham Joshua Heschel wrote, "I did not ask for success; I asked for wonder. And you gave it to me."[3]

Give us today our daily bread.

In 1922, the tomb of the Egyptian Pharaoh, Tutankhamun, was discovered by archaeologists. Tutankhamun lived and died about 1300 years before Christ. One reason Tutankhamun is famous is because, when his tomb was discovered, it was found largely intact. The world was able to see the inner workings of an ancient civilization and some of its vast riches.

One year, I was in Melbourne, Australia, and an exhibition of some of Tutankhamun's treasures were on display. They had been transported from Egypt especially. I wandered through room after room full of all kinds of wonderful objects. All of them were of immeasurable worth. I was in awe at the craftmanship and the engraving, of the shapes in gold and other precious metals – all from three thousand years ago. While there was so much to see, this was only a small sample of all that had been found in the tomb. Most of it was still back in Egypt.

Finally, I came to the end of the display and walked out into a shop. The shop was full of Tutankhamun-themed souvenirs. I had just spent over an hour walking through a display of some of the treasures from a king's tomb, and I

---

2. Ignatius of Loyola (c. 1491/93–1556).
3. Heschel, *I Asked for Wonder*, 7.

was now invited to purchase material items to remind me of the experience. It was then I was struck by a powerful contrast. I had just seen the vast rich stores of a king's tomb, yet the only thing found in the King of kings' tomb were his grave clothes (John 20:5–7). The contrast was breathtaking. Not only that, but the King of kings emptied himself of his riches and became one of us (Phil 2:6–7). Jesus emptied himself of the extravagance of heaven to embrace the poverty of earth.

Give us today our daily bread.

So, when Peter makes his statement on our behalf, "We have left all we had to follow you!," it is said to the one who left all he had so that "no one who has left home or wife or brothers or sisters or parents or children for the sake of the kingdom of God will fail to receive many times as much in this age, and in the age to come eternal life."

Give us today our daily bread.

Reflection

What reward and recognition do you expect for following Jesus? Are your expectations more in line with the Apostle Paul or the Prodigal Son's brother?

Pray

Give us today our daily bread.

6

Forgive Us Our Debts as We Also Have Forgiven Our Debtors
A Prayer for Preachers Wanting Understanding

Luke 18:31–34

Jesus took the Twelve aside and told them, "We are going up to Jerusalem, and everything that is written by the prophets about the Son of Man will be fulfilled. He will be delivered over to the Gentiles. They will mock him, insult him and spit on him; they will flog him and kill him. On the third day he will rise again."

The disciples did not understand any of this. Its meaning was hidden from them, and they did not know what he was talking about.

A comedian once wrote, "All humour is at someone's expense." I read that comment over thirty-five years ago and it has stayed with me. The person paying the price of the humour can be the person hearing the joke, telling the joke or a person or group not present. The quote has not stopped me enjoying or making humour, but it has influenced my use of humour. Sometimes the quote has stopped me from making a joke that would have hurt someone else. Other times I have thought about it only when it was too late. I have made a humourous comment and then remembered, "All humour is at someone's expense." The person listening, or even people not there, paid a price. That is never a nice feeling.

"All humour is at someone's expense."

If all humour is at someone's expense, how much more is forgiveness?

All forgiveness is at someone's expense.

Think of times when you have asked for forgiveness. That requires you to acknowledge your wrongdoing and humble yourself before God or others. You are confronted by your failing. Asking for forgiveness is costly.

Think of times when you have granted forgiveness. That requires you to loosen your grip of the offence against you and let it slide from your grasp. It is as if your hands let go of the hurt so that your hands are free to take the other person's hand in a sign of peace. Granting forgiveness is costly.

Forgive us our debts, as we also have forgiven our debtors.

In the portion of Scripture before us, Luke 18:31–34, we see the ultimate cost of forgiveness. Jesus describes his suffering in detail. Jesus speaks of where, why and how he will suffer.

- Where: In Jerusalem, the city of God.
- Why: In fulfilment of the Scriptures which speak of the redemption of God.
- How: He will be handed over to the Romans and the details of his death are described.

Jesus finishes the description with a statement of certainty, "On the third day he will rise again" (Luke 18:33). Luke, the gospel writer, finishes the description by stating the disciples' confusion: "The disciples did not understand any of this. Its meaning was hidden from them, and they did not know what he was talking about" (Luke 18:34).

This captures the difficulties and mysteries we face as we seek to live a life marked by the redemption and forgiveness of God. On the one hand, the words from Luke 18 give us a clear picture of the mystery of God's forgiveness. We see Jesus's suffering, death and resurrection. We understand this is God's way of dealing with humanity's sin. On the other hand, the words from Luke 18 give us a realistic picture of the mystery of God's forgiveness. We see Jesus's suffering, death and resurrection. Yet we do not fully understand how this is God's way of dealing with humanity's sin:

> Beyond all question, the mystery from which true godliness springs is great:

> He appeared in the flesh,
> was vindicated by the Spirit,
> was seen by angels,
> was preached among the nations,
> was believed on in the world,
> was taken up in glory. (1 Tim 3:16)

Perhaps it is fair to say there are days when we find ourselves in the clarity of Luke 18:31–33, where we understand the nature of the suffering, death and resurrection of Jesus. Then there are days when we find ourselves in the confusion of Luke 18:34, where, like the Twelve, we do not understand.

Luke 18:31–34 acts like a map in our journey of coming to a place of forgiveness. The verses describing the detail of Jesus's suffering and death (Luke 18:31–33) show the cost. We see there is a journey. The verse speaking of his resurrection (Luke 18:33) gives us a vision of a restored life. We see the destination. The last verse (Luke 18:34) shows us our limitations. We can be at times lost in it all.

When I was training to be a pastor, the person in charge of my training told a story about when he was a hospital chaplain. He visited the same female patient several times. During each visit she would tell him the identical story. She talked about a time when she had done something wrong. Each time she told the story, it was as if she was telling him for the first time. After hearing the story several times, the chaplain began to feel frustrated. During one visit, as she was telling him the story yet again, the chaplain's frustration spilled out. He said to her bluntly, "You are forgiven!" The woman grabbed him by the shoulders and pulled him in so that they were very close – face-to-face. She then said with great feeling, "Thank you, God! Thank you, God! Thank you, God!"

Here was someone who was certain God can forgive but was lost trying to reach the certainty of that forgiveness. The chaplain was left with the experience of the mystery of forgiveness in that he had been the agent for it.

Forgive us our debts, as we also have forgiven our debtors.

In my first year as a pastor, I was astounded by what church members confessed to me. People I barely knew asked to see me. They told me about secret sins they had held in their hearts for years. Each person basically said the same thing: "As our pastor, I think you should know." What surprised me was they had prayed for God's forgiveness, yet still felt the need to confess it to me. Again, this emphasized the clarity and confusion that people can strike in experiencing forgiveness.

But what about you as a preacher? What about those times when you know the story of how forgiveness has come about (Luke 18:31–33), yet you are like the Twelve, uncertain about its outworking in your life (Luke 18:34)? The way Luke 18:31–34 is written accurately sums up difficult seasons preachers can experience. They can preach with passion and precision the contours of the gospel. They can preach verses 31 to 33 and tell their congregations about what happened to Jesus in Jerusalem. They can preach about his trial, the mocking and insults he endured and the physical suffering. They can describe the horror of the crucifixion and the stunning joy of the resurrection. But while they preach this gospel, they secretly experience the turmoil of verse 34: the meaning is hidden from them. That is a heavy burden to carry, especially when you stand before people to preach the word of God. I have spoken with preachers who secretly carry the shame of their sinful acts and struggle to know the liberating effect of Jesus's forgiveness. When they preach, they are sincere about what they say but they feel hollow. In fact, there are some topics and parts of Scripture they cannot preach because they feel hypocritical doing so.

As a pastor, I once went through a season when I felt I was under the judgement of God. I could not get rid of the feeling of dread. I felt God was somehow judging me. I did not know the reason why I felt this way. I knew the gospel of forgiveness, but for some reason, I could not experience it. You could say, I knew Luke 18:31–33 but I was experiencing Luke 18:34. Finally, I spoke with a Christian leader I met with regularly. I said, "I don't know why, but I feel like God is judging me. I know what I would say to encourage someone if they were experiencing the same thing; but it makes no difference. I cannot get rid of the feeling that I am under the judgement of God." The Christian leader smiled and simply said, "It's funny isn't it? How the cross wasn't enough." His point was playfully and powerfully made. The sense of dread and fear lifted immediately. Of course the cross is enough. I had somehow lost sight and memory of that.

There are times as preachers when it is easier to preach about forgiveness than experience it for ourselves. There are times when preachers are isolated from the very message of forgiveness they preach.

Forgive us our debts, as we also have forgiven our debtors.

In a cathedral in Edinburgh, Scotland, there hangs a huge painting entitled "The Presence."[1] The painting is of the inside of the cathedral as if you were standing at the very back. The painting depicts the inside of the cathedral mainly in darkness, but at the front in the distance, the communion table is bathed in golden light. Worshippers are gathered around the table participating in the Lord's Supper. Nearly all the chairs in the cathedral are empty because nearly everyone is at the Lord's Table. However, at the back, in the dim light, one of the empty chairs is turned slightly towards the side and back. Someone has left their seat but not walked forward to communion. As you look at the

---

1. The painting was painted by Edinburgh artist A. E. Borthwick in 1910. It hangs in St Mary's Episcopal (Scottish Anglican) Cathedral.

painting, there she is. She is kneeling in distress at the foot of one of the rear great stone pillars beside her empty seat. She is alone, in anguish and separate from those at the front who are taking the bread and cup of the Lord's Supper. Who knows what keeps her from joining her brothers and sisters in Christ. But her posture speaks of one trying to find peace with their God. She is on her knees, hands gripped together in anguished prayer. She is isolated. Her posture looks like that of many preachers who have a public ministry to fulfil but are torn by private pain. However, she is not entirely alone. Just to one side of her is the illuminated presence of Christ. He is holding out his hand towards her in a gesture of comfort and blessing. In the darkness, he sees her. At first glance it seems as if Jesus is standing by her. But he's not. He is walking past her. For, in the murky darkness, and in the midst of the empty chairs, there appear to be others like her. Two or three other people who are also shrouded in darkness and who knows what anguish. They too have not joined the majority at the Lord's Table. But they too will soon know the Presence.

Perhaps that is you seated alone in the darkness.

Forgive us our debts, as we also have forgiven our debtors.

May you too know that the cross is enough. May you too know the presence of the resurrected Christ.

Reflection

What area in your life are you struggling to know the forgiveness of God?

Pray

Forgive us our debts, as we also have forgiven our debtors.

7

Lead Us Not into Temptation
A Prayer for Preachers Wanting Healing

Luke 18:35–43

As Jesus approached Jericho, a blind man was sitting by the roadside begging. When he heard the crowd going by, he asked what was happening. They told him, "Jesus of Nazareth is passing by."

He called out, "Jesus, Son of David, have mercy on me!"

Those who led the way rebuked him and told him to be quiet, but he shouted all the more, "Son of David, have mercy on me!"

Jesus stopped and ordered the man to be brought to him. When he came near, Jesus asked him, "What do you want me to do for you?"

"Lord, I want to see," he replied.

Jesus said to him, "Receive your sight; your faith has healed you." Immediately he received his sight and followed Jesus, praising God. When all the people saw it, they also praised God.

Preaching is hard. Whether you preach occasionally or regularly, you will find that writing a sermon can be a battle. I like how one author and teacher of preaching describes the struggle: "Someone must suffer for the sermon. If it is not the preacher who is willing to pay the price then it will be the congregation."[1] The battle can take any number of forms. The battle can be trying to find the central idea of the portion of Scripture you are preaching from. Or, it might be the distractions you fight as you try to concentrate long

---
1. Larsen, *Anatomy of Preaching*, 89.

enough to write the sermon. Sometimes the battle will be finding illustrations and applications which are true to the Bible passage. You struggle to create a sermon which is clear and relevant for your listeners, and time is running out before you preach it. Such battles are usually unseen by many, yet as the quote above makes clear, if the battle is not won by the preacher then the congregation will pay the price. As hard as these battles can be, they are a normal part of preaching. They are fought sermon by sermon.

However, there is another kind of battle for the preacher. This battle is not fought sermon by sermon but week by week, month by month and, for some preachers, year by year. This battle is difficult to describe, but it involves a slow loss of sight. The preacher battles the temptation to commit less time for their own spiritual growth and prayerful sermon preparation. One writer describes what the temptation can look like:

> As the pressures of parish [church] life mount and the "urgent" supplants what is genuinely important, we say, "Well, it won't hurt if just *this* week I don't spend quite as much time on sermon preparation." And lo and behold, we were absolutely right! They love us anyway! "Good sermon," they continue to chime at the door. Week by week we learn to get by with less and less text study, prayer, and reflection.[2]

While the battle can be difficult to define, its effects are obvious: the preacher slowly loses their spiritual sight. The temptation to study and pray less becomes stronger the longer we think no-one notices. The temptation to take shortcuts in our sermon preparation becomes more attractive each time such a sermon appears to have a good effect on people. If these temptations become our habit, one day we will discover we have become spiritually blind.

Lead us not into temptation.

In Luke 18:35–43, we have the picture of a blind man sitting on the roadside begging. Jesus, in the midst of a crowd, is going by. The blind man begging serves as a picture of the preacher who has become spiritually blind. Such a preacher has slowly lost the ability to see things in Scripture and they feel like they need to beg for something – for anything – to be able to write their next sermon.

The story in Luke 18 is desperate and urgent. So is the state of the preacher who has said yes to the temptation to do less and less about their spiritual formation and sermon preparation.

---

2. Nieman, "Preaching that Drives People," 248. Emphasis in original.

The blind man speaks for any preacher who realizes they have become like a blind beggar. Questions lurk in the heart and mind of such preachers: Am I losing the ability to preach? How long before those I preach to realize I am blind? Will I ever see again?

In Luke 18, the blind man hears a crowd going by and he asks what is happening. He is told, "Jesus of Nazareth is passing by" (Luke 18:36–37). For the preacher who has lost their sight, such an answer can sound like good news or bad news.

Good news: Jesus is drawing near and coming close to where I am. "Maybe this is a sign that God has remembered me."

Bad news: Jesus is passing by and not stopping where I am. "Maybe this is a sign God has forgotten me."

Whether you think it is good news or bad news, the blind beggar gifts us a prayer: "Jesus, Son of David, have mercy on me!" (Luke 18:38). However, the other voices threaten to drown out his voice. Those who led the crowd rebuked him and told him to be quiet (Luke 18:39). For preachers who have lost their sight, it is easy to allow such voices to have their way. Such voices can take the form of regret or guilt about how we have allowed ourselves to get to such a spiritual state. We hear inner voices shout, "Keep quiet! You have no right to ask for help." We hear external voices as we listen to people speak of their faithfulness to their ministry in Christ. The effect of hearing such testimonies silences us because, by comparison, we are ashamed because we have been unfaithful. We sit on the roadside having lost sight of our ministry in Christ. We are tempted to do what the voices rebuke us to do: keep quiet.

Lead us not into temptation.

The blind beggar is our inspiration. Instead of being quiet he becomes louder: "Son of David, have mercy on me!" (Luke 18:39). In using the title "Son of David," he appeals to the royalty and kingship of Jesus the Messiah. He appeals to the One who has authority to grant mercy. Jesus hears the cry, and in Luke 18:40–41, there is a beautiful pause in the story and in the man's life. In contrast to the initial description of the crowd, and Jesus passing by, we read that "Jesus stopped and ordered the man to be brought to him" (Luke 18:40). Throughout Scripture, this is the habit of God. God hears and stops to attend to the cry for mercy. We see it in the history of Israel from the exodus onwards. We see it in gospel narratives such as Mark 5:25–34, when Jesus stops for the woman who touched the hem of his cloak. We see it in Matthew 15:21–28, when the Canaanite woman cried out, nearly word-for-word, the same prayer as the blind beggar. Do you believe you will see it in your life? Do not fall into the temptation of listening to those voices which say otherwise.

Lead us not into temptation.

The blind beggar is brought before Jesus, and Jesus asks, "What do you want me to do for you?" (Luke 18:41). Jesus's question appears to be unnecessary. Surely he knew the man was blind. However, there is something necessary and life-giving in simply asking what we require from Jesus. The blind beggar gifts us a second prayer, "Lord, I want to see" (Luke 18:41).

For you who struggle with a slow loss of sight as a preacher, do these words offer you a way to regain your sight?

They did for me.

I read this story in Luke 18 at a time when I felt I was losing my spiritual insight into the Scriptures and my abilities as a preacher. I had been fearing such blindness and loss for several months. When I read the blind man's request, "Lord I want to see," I realized this was my prayer. I began to pray this short prayer regularly. One month later, I travelled to Hyderabad, India, to conduct a Langham Preaching event with Paul Windsor (International Director of Langham Preaching). I always travel with a Bible verse to sustain me and the blind man's prayer was such a verse on this occasion. After all, I still needed to regain my sight.

When I arrived at the training venue, Paul had already been there for several days training another group. About thirty minutes after I arrived, Paul finished teaching a class and said to me, "I want to show you something, but you have to close your eyes." He then led me outside and instructed me to close my eyes. He walked ahead and I, with my eyes closed, followed with my hand on his shoulder to guide me. Paul said, "This must look unusual." But I was already thinking, "This is the story of Luke 18 being acted out! I am in the blind man's story!"

After several moments of walking, he told me to open my eyes. There before us, in a big courtyard, were a series of large stones arranged in a half-circle pattern. Each stone was similar: there was a bronze-like sculpture set into the stone and, beneath the sculpture, a verse from Genesis 1–2 recounting the days of creation. Alongside each verse from Genesis there was a matching verse, mostly from the book of Revelation, about the promised new creation. There they were: one large stone, with its accompanying image, for each of the days of creation, and the whole biblical story represented by verses from the first and last book of the Bible.

The scales began to fall from my eyes.

Paul then led me across the courtyard to the next sculpture. This is why he had told me to close my eyes. We had walked past it to get to the stones, and if I had seen this next sculpture, the story would have been spoiled.

For now before me was another verse set on a sign, "Then the eyes of them were opened (Gen 3:7)." On the ground was a sculpture of a person lying face down in a despairing and distressed state. The person's head was buried in their hands. The figure spoke a single word: anguish. In front of the figure were two pieces of fruit with a bite out of each. In the middle of the figure's body was a deep hole – the effect of rebelling against God's command to not take from the tree of the knowledge of good and evil (Gen 2:16–17).

Then Paul directed me to look beyond this figure which represented the fallen human race. There above the main entrance to the training venue was a Bible verse in gold lettering: "All the families of the earth will be blessed through you (Gen 12:3)." The great promise to Abraham and the great promise all can benefit from.

So, there in a wonderful triangle of biblical testimony were the days of creation from Genesis and the new creation in Revelation, the awful reality and reminder of the effects of sin and God's wonderful promise of how he will redeem his creation.

I was astounded. My prayer, "Lord I want to see," was answered. Then Paul, totally unaware of what I had been praying for the past month and the last few minutes, said to me, "I wanted you to see it." I heard Paul say the words, but I felt the Spirit of God had authored them.

Over the next few mornings, very early each day, I sat on one of the seats set up in the midst of the stones telling the creation story. I sat literally surrounded by the overall sweep of the biblical story from Genesis to Revelation. From there I could also see the promise of Genesis 12:3 above the main entrance of the venue and the place where Genesis 3:7 was represented. I was surrounded by the complete biblical story of creation, fall and redemption. My sight as a preacher was regained. However, with it came a warning. I noted that between each of the stone sculptures were plants. Yet, these plants were not only beautiful to look at, they were full of large and sharp thorns. The presence of these thorns planted in the midst of the Genesis and Revelation verses reminded me of the parable of the Sower (Mark 4:1–20). Perhaps one reason I had lost my sight as a preacher was because of "thorns" choking the word in my life. In particular, the worries of this life (Mark 4:19).

Lead us not into temptation.

As my eyes grew accustomed again to the biblical story, the ending of the story in Luke 18 landed in my soul (Luke 18:42–43): "Jesus said to him, 'Receive your sight; your faith has healed you.' Immediately he received his sight and followed Jesus, praising God. When all the people saw it, they also praised God." These words of Jesus not only speak healing to blind begging preachers, they are also spoken in an affirming way. Jesus expresses pleasure in his words, "Your faith has healed you." Contained in his affirmation is the sense that your pursuit and desire for God is in itself pleasing to God. You have cried out to Christ for mercy and sight. With pleasure Jesus stops, calls you and declares, "Receive your sight; your faith has healed you."

This leads to a renewing and deepening of your commitment to follow Jesus and, for those who hear of your testimony, a reason to praise God.

Reflection

Answer Jesus's question: "What do you want me to do for you?"

Pray

Lead us not into temptation.

8

Deliver Us from the Evil One
A Prayer for Preachers Wanting Restoration

Luke 19:1–10

Jesus entered Jericho and was passing through. A man was there by the name of Zacchaeus; he was a chief tax collector and was wealthy. He wanted to see who Jesus was, but because he was short he could not see over the crowd. So he ran ahead and climbed a sycamore-fig tree to see him, since Jesus was coming that way.

When Jesus reached the spot, he looked up and said to him, "Zacchaeus, come down immediately. I must stay at your house today." So he came down at once and welcomed him gladly.

All the people saw this and began to mutter, "He has gone to be the guest of a sinner."

But Zacchaeus stood up and said to the Lord, "Look, Lord! Here and now I give half of my possessions to the poor, and if I have cheated anybody out of anything, I will pay back four times the amount."

Jesus said to him, "Today salvation has come to this house, because this man, too, is a son of Abraham. For the Son of Man came to seek and to save the lost."

Jericho stands as an obstacle to approaching God. Jericho appears early in the Bible and has a prominent place in the story of the exodus. Jericho entered Israel's story when Israel arrived at the frontier of the promised land having been led by Moses for forty years in the wilderness. Across the river Jordan, Jericho stood as a fortress city blocking Israel's entry into the promised land. Before his death, and before Israel attempted to cross the Jordan, Moses commissioned Joshua as the new leader of Israel. Joshua followed God's instructions and conquered Jericho (Josh 6). After its destruction, Joshua pronounced a curse on anyone who attempted to rebuild the city (Josh 6:26). He did not want this obstacle to exist again. About five hundred years later, a man named Hiel of Bethel rebuilt Jericho and Joshua's curse was visited on Hiel's family (1 Kgs 16:34). Two of his sons died during the reconstruction of the city. So Jericho does not enjoy a positive picture in the biblical story. Jericho stands as an obstacle to approaching God. Now, in Luke 19, Jesus, a new Joshua, enters the city of Jericho. Within this city, Jesus confronts obstacles stopping someone from approaching God.

The story focuses on a citizen of that city: Zacchaeus. The way Zacchaeus is introduced is important. We are told his name, occupation and sin (Luke 19:2). His name means "pure, clean, innocent," but Zacchaeus is corrupt. He gains wealth by cheating others as a tax collector. He takes more money than is required and gains great wealth at the expense of those he taxes. The depth of his sin is highlighted in that he is not described as a tax collector but as a "chief tax collector" – the only time the term is used in the Bible. There is a deep divide between the meaning of Zacchaeus's name and who he has become. For his character is not pure, clean or innocent. Zacchaeus has departed from his named identity as a person. He has betrayed his people, his God and himself. Zacchaeus is a person of prominence and power but also a person whose life is tainted by sin and shame. The divide between the meaning of Zacchaeus's name and who he has become is seen in the crowd's name for him: sinner (Luke 19:7).

In Jericho, Zacchaeus is both prominent and isolated from the community. His position is such that everyone knows him, but no one wants anything to do with him. Evil has fragmented his personality. Evil has built up obstacles hindering him from approaching God. Zacchaeus is lost.

In Luke 18 we have the following stories:

- A parable about a widow trying to get justice from an unjust judge (Luke 18:1–8).
- A parable about a Pharisee and tax collector praying in the temple (Luke 18:9–14).
- A story about children being stopped by the disciples from seeing Jesus (Luke 18:15–17).
- A story about a rich ruler who cannot follow Jesus because of his wealth (Luke 18:18–30).
- A story of a blind beggar crying out to Jesus (Luke 18:35–43).

It is as if, in Luke 19:1–10, these stories are sewn into a garment used to clothe Zacchaeus: it is a perfect fit. All the stories in Luke 18 of people encountering obstacles in approaching God are visited upon Zacchaeus.[1] Zacchaeus represents them all:

- He is like the widow obstructed by an unjust judge.
- He is like the tax collector in the temple judged by the Pharisee.
- He is like the children trying to get to Jesus but kept back by others.
- He is like the rich ruler blinded by his riches and kept from the kingdom.
- He is like the blind beggar kept from seeing Jesus because of a physical limitation.

Zacchaeus is lost and he knows it.

The story of Zacchaeus communicates his desperation to see Jesus. The opening verses describe lots of movement and action. The story is fast paced. Jesus is passing through Jericho (Luke 19:1), so there is limited opportunity for Zacchaeus to encounter him. Zacchaeus is short in height, and the crowd hinders his attempts to see Jesus (Luke 19:3). Time is running out. Jesus is passing through Jericho but not staying. So, Zacchaeus runs ahead and climbs a tree (Luke 19:4). The rabbis had a saying: "A man's manner of walking tells you what he is."[2] Men dressed in robes, so to run would require them to lift their robes and be undignified. Therefore, men of dignity and honour would not run and would definitely not climb a tree. But Zacchaeus is lost and desperate and would rather run and climb than risk missing seeing Jesus.

Then the pace of the story changes. Whereas the frantic pace highlighted Zacchaeus attempting to see Jesus, now the pace highlights Jesus's desire to see Zacchaeus. Jesus arrives at the place where Zacchaeus is in the tree and looks up. Jesus says, "Zacchaeus, come down immediately. I must stay at your house today" (Luke 19:5). Jesus's desire to meet with Zacchaeus is divine intervention. In the Gospel of Luke, Jesus often used the word "must" to communicate something his Father required him to do.[3] Zacchaeus comes down quickly and welcomes Jesus into his home. The description of Zacchaeus's enthusiasm to see Jesus (e.g. "ran ahead"; "climbed"; "came down at once") is now matched with descriptions of Zacchaeus's enthusiastic response to Jesus. Zacchaeus stands before Jesus and declares he will give half his possessions to the poor

---

1. Green, *Gospel of Luke*, 666–667.
2. Bailey, *Finding the Lost*, 144.
3. Takatemjen, "Luke," 1373.

and, in line with the law of Moses, repay four times anything he has cheated anyone (Luke 19:8). He makes this declaration at a time in history when rabbis considered giving 20 percent to the poor more than enough. Jesus then matches Zacchaeus's declaration with one of his own.

Jesus declares that salvation has come to Zacchaeus's home, that Zacchaeus is part of the family of God and that the "Son of Man came to seek and to save the lost" (Luke 19:10). Jesus reverses the effect of evil in Zacchaeus's life. He names Zacchaeus as a "Son of Abraham" (Luke 19:9) and restores him to the family of God. Zacchaeus reverses the effects of evil by restoring to the community what he has taken. The obstacles have been removed. Zacchaeus is found.

Deliver us from the evil one.

As a preacher, whether you preach often or not, you are in a position of prominence in the congregation. Unfortunately, in churches throughout the world, there have been examples of preachers taking advantage of the people they are supposed to serve. Some preachers gain wealth, control church decisions for their own benefit, demand they are the "Lord's anointed" and their authority should not be questioned. Some enter into inappropriate relationships. Like Zacchaeus, they become removed from their identity in God, and there is a deep division within their life. Like Zacchaeus, they take more than is required or is acceptable. Like Zacchaeus, they become isolated from the family of God. Like Zacchaeus, obstacles grow, hindering their approach to God. Like Zacchaeus, they are lost.

Deliver us from the evil one.

But like Zacchaeus, their lives can become marked with a growing sense of desperation to see Jesus. Just as Zacchaeus was on that day in Jericho, they are afraid Jesus is passing by and not staying. Similar to how events unfolded in Luke 19:1–10, their attempt to see Jesus is hindered by obstacles only truly known to themselves. They are deeply aware of how far they have fallen from their true identity in God; of the depth of their sin and shame; of how disconnected from their community they are. They want to see Christ again, and so, in their own way, they run ahead and climb trees in a desperate attempt to catch a glimpse of him. Even if it is undignified. For they can relate to the experience of Zacchaeus when it feels like every obstacle possible hinders their path to redemption.

We, too, can look at the stories of obstacles recorded in Luke 18 and feel their reality. Like Zacchaeus, it is as if we are clothed with them. Like the persistent widow, we might encounter the refusal of help from someone who has the power to give it. Or like the tax collector in the temple, we bear the condemnation of those who consider themselves more righteous. Like the children stopped from approaching Jesus, we might be discouraged by other disciples saying we are bothering Jesus. Or, like the rich ruler, we are stalled by our attachment to wealth and influence. Like the blind man, perhaps we are restricted by physical limitations and our difficulties are increased by people not helping us to overcome those limitations. We feel deeply divided within ourselves and feel disconnected from God and his community.

Deliver us from the evil one.

Along with such feelings and in the presence of such obstacles, are we prepared to speak words of confession and offer works of restitution? And herein lies the challenge: being willing and able to speak words from the heart and make compensation with a generous heart. There is a place – indeed, a need – for preachers who have lost their way to be prepared to apologise to the people they have betrayed. Such apologies will involve careful words and courageous actions. All in response to the Son of Man who comes to seek and save the lost.

Deliver us from the evil one.

I was a police chaplain for five years. A police chaplain helps the police and their families in much the same way a pastor cares for his or her congregation. I would offer counselling, provide training to help police cope with their work, and conduct weddings and funerals. One night I went out on patrol, and the two police officers I was with were called to a domestic violence incident. It was 3:00 a.m. on a dark and stormy winter night. When we arrived at the home, we found a woman with blood on her face from being punched by her male partner. One of the officers took her into another room so she could tell him what happened without being heard by her partner. The male offender, the other police officer and I waited together. The offender did not know I was a chaplain; he thought I was a detective.

Eventually the police officer came out of the room after talking with the injured woman. He told the other police officer to arrest the male offender and take him to the police car. He told me to accompany them and wait in the car. So, the three of us sat in the police car while the other officer continued to get a statement from the woman. The offender and police officer were in the back of the car and I sat in the front. No one said a word. We sat in silence. I thought, "How on earth could the light of Christ ever penetrate a place like this? How could Christ ever impact a person like this? How on earth could the message of light ever be heard here?!" The darkness of the night and stormy weather seemed to confirm the apparent impossibility of the light of Christ penetrating such a situation. The obstacles that were in the way of this man encountering Christ seemed impossibly huge.

I had no sooner finished thinking this than the offender broke the silence (remember, he thought I was a detective). He said, "You know – I used to be a pastor." Then he began to talk about his ministry and the work of the Holy Spirit that he had seen during that time. I sat in that police car in awe. Here I was thinking that this man was out of reach of God, and then I am listening to him testify to the work of God in his life from years past. I do not know what prompted him to speak this way to a uniformed police officer and a man he assumed was a detective. But, for me, Jesus was saying, "For the Son of Man came to seek and to save what was lost." Or, more to the point, answering the prayer "Deliver us from the evil one."

Reflection

What obstacle in your life stops you from approaching God? What do you need to confess and make restitution for?

Pray

Deliver us from the evil one.

Part II

The Lord's Prayer as Heard in Jesus's Death

The Cries from the Cross

9

Our Father in Heaven
A Prayer for Preachers Needing Reassurance

Mark 15:33–39

At noon, darkness came over the whole land until three in the afternoon. And at three in the afternoon Jesus cried out in a loud voice, "Eloi, Eloi, lema sabachthani?" (which means "My God, my God, why have you forsaken me?").

When some of those standing near heard this, they said, "Listen, he's calling Elijah."

Someone ran, filled a sponge with wine vinegar, put it on a staff, and offered it to Jesus to drink. "Now leave him alone. Let's see if Elijah comes to take him down," he said.

With a loud cry, Jesus breathed his last.

The curtain of the temple was torn in two from top to bottom. And when the centurion, who stood there in front of Jesus, saw how he died, he said, "Surely this man was the Son of God!"

Before using this portion of Scripture to reflect on our ministry, we need to first acknowledge the mystery and uniqueness of what is described. Jesus's desperate cry of despair to his Father is a mystery. Such is the divine depth of their relationship that it is beyond human understanding. God the Son cries out to God the Father. Jesus's cry laments a fracture in their relationship. This is mysterious. "However this central cry of Jesus is understood, it remains mysteriously true that in Jesus's death as well as during his life, 'God was in Christ' (2 Cor 5:19), present and active."[1]

---

1. Harris, *Seven Sayings*, 69.

Our Father in heaven.

Jesus's desperate cry of despair to his Father is unique. Given who Jesus is and his work on the cross, his cry is the expression of such deep torment that no human can lay claim to the same experience. "Christ was forsaken by God so that believers may never be forsaken by him, either during life or after death (cf. Rom 8:35–39; Heb 13:5–6)."[2]

So we engage with this cry from the cross with humility. At a mysterious and unique level, Jesus's cry was from him alone to his Father, "My God, my God. . . ." Jesus's cry speaks of his great spiritual and physical anguish. So we engage with this cry from the cross with thankfulness.

At another level, Jesus's cry was for us to his Father: Our Father in heaven. Jesus's cry speaks for us in times of great spiritual and physical anguish.

As such, this moment can be seen through the lens of Hebrews 4:15–16:

> For we do not have a high priest who is unable to empathize with our weaknesses, but we have one who has been tempted in every way, just as we are – yet he did not sin. Let us then approach God's throne of grace with confidence, so that we may receive mercy and find grace to help us in our time of need.

Jesus's cry from the cross to our Father in heaven is a prayer of our high priest. This prayer leads to mercy and grace in our time of need. Especially when, as a preacher, you experience times of abandonment in your preaching ministry. Whether your preaching ministry involves you preaching occasionally or regularly, there is no difference. Whether you preach as a member of a church or as the pastor of a church, there is no difference. The spiritual anguish is deep, and your prayers seem unanswered. The sense of isolation is strong, and the season is dark. You are unsure how long this will last or – worse still – whether you will last.

Our Father in heaven.

Listen to Jesus's cry, "My God, my God, why have you forsaken me?" This cry leads us to our Father in heaven. The cry – "My God, my God, why have you forsaken me?" – is the opening phrase of Psalm 22. Other descriptions of the crucifixion echo parts of Psalm 22 (e.g. Jesus's thirst, the mocking, the physical suffering, the dividing of his clothes and casting lots for his garment), but this cry is the clearest and most exact reference to Psalm 22. These words draw us to this Psalm, and they serve as a gateway to the rest of the Psalm which deepens the meaning of what Jesus cried out in a loud voice:

---

2. Harris, 69.

> My God, my God, why have you forsaken me?
> Why are you so far from saving me,
> so far from my cries of anguish?
> My God, I cry out by day, but you do not answer,
> by night, but I find no rest. (Ps 22:1–2)

In using the words of Psalm 22, Jesus's cry is a prayer. He was at the extreme moment of the crucifixion: at the end of six hours on the cross and three hours of darkness over the land. A darkness which conveys the curse and horror of sin upon the world. A darkness which is oppressive and all-consuming. A darkness like that when God judged Egypt before the Passover; a "darkness that can be felt" (Exod 10:21). From within this darkness, Jesus's prayer contains language of abandonment and yet is said in a spirit of trust, "My God, my God . . ." Even though there was no answer from heaven, the Son calls out of the darkness to the Father still trusting in "my God." In the apparent vacuum of being forsaken, Jesus still addresses his Father intimately. In the immediate absence of an answer or action from heaven, Jesus still addresses his Father as "My God." This is our inspiration. In reflecting on this word from the cross, one Bible commentator observes, "One of Satan's most important tasks . . . is to convince people that God has abandoned them, so that they curse him and die."[3] Satan fails in his task here.

Our Father in heaven.

In the midst of your anguish, when there seems no answer or action from heaven, Jesus has empowered us to pray "Our Father in heaven." From the midst of the darkness overshadowing you, here is a prayer which is intimate and trusting. Even in the absence of an immediate answer from your Father in heaven, he remains "Our Father in heaven." This is your prayer even when it seems our Father in heaven is not answering but those on earth around us are.

After Jesus cried out in a loud voice, others standing near did answer. Some said, "Listen, he's calling Elijah" (Mark 15:35). We do not know whether they misheard the words "Eloi, eloi" (Mark 15:34) as "Elijah" or whether they were drawing on the Jewish expectation that Elijah would come to help the righteous in times of need. In any case, even if the offer of wine vinegar was an attempt to give comfort, the words were cruel. "Now leave him alone. Let's see if Elijah comes to take him down" (Mark 15:36). Jesus was isolated, and in a way, these words put him on trial again. Will there be divine intervention for him? By contrast, there was another person who answered: "And when the centurion,

---

3. Marcus, *Mark 8–16*, 1063.

who stood there in front of Jesus, saw how he died, he said, 'Surely this man was the Son of God!'" (Mark 15:39). One, who was familiar with the faith, was saying Jesus was not of God. The other – and it is reasonable to assume the centurion was pagan – attested that Jesus was of God.

In times of anguish and darkness, as you await an answer from our Father in heaven, the voices around you have the potential to add to your pain while others might relieve it. Some answers may be cruel while others might be unexpectedly life-giving. Both disappointment and encouragement can come from unexpected sources. As you try and reach God from the darkness, crying, "My God, my God – our Father in heaven – why do you not answer?!," it is as if you have some in the church offering cruel words, and those who do not know God offering words of affirmation.

Our Father in heaven.

When I was pastoring a church, we had a major crisis in our life as a congregation. During that crisis, one night after a worship service, a married couple who were members of the church asked to speak with me. They began to severely criticize how I and the church elders were managing the crisis. Finally, after I thought I had heard what they needed to say, I said, "I'm sorry. But I need to stop this conversation. I don't have the emotional energy to continue it." This was the first and only time I stopped a pastoral conversation in my time as a pastor. The wife immediately said, "We don't mean any of this personally against you." Her husband quickly said to her, "Yes we do!" I actually experienced physical pain in my spirit from their attack.

In contrast, in the midst of the crisis, I had to contact several non-Christian families in the wider community. They had teenagers coming to the church even though the parents were not attending. I needed to inform these parents about the crisis. I dreaded the reaction I would receive. However, without exception, every response was warm, compassionate and gentle. These non-Christians thanked me for contacting them and spoke words of encouragement about the church's ministry in the wider community.

It was as if some within the church stood back to see if God would save the situation: like those offering wine vinegar. While those not part of the church stood in front of us and said, "Surely God is with you," like the Roman centurion.

When your darkness is made worse by those you least expected it from, the challenge is to not allow a root of bitterness to spring up. Their life, and yours, depends on it: "Make every effort to live in peace with everyone and to be holy; without holiness no one will see the Lord. See to it that no one falls short of the grace of God and that no bitter root grows up to cause trouble and defile many" (Heb 12:14–15).

Our Father in heaven.

The apostle Paul illustrates the kind of spirit necessary in the presence of such abandonment in ministry:

> At my first defense, no one came to my support, but everyone deserted me. May it not be held against them. But the Lord stood at my side and gave me strength, so that through me the message might be fully proclaimed and all the Gentiles might hear it. And I was delivered from the lion's mouth. The Lord will rescue me from every evil attack and will bring me safely to his heavenly kingdom. To him be glory for ever and ever. Amen. (2 Tim 4:16–18)

In the disappointment of being alone in the darkness, Paul trusts the Lord and endeavours to keep relationship with those who abandoned him. He does not want their failure held against them. He shows no bitterness towards them but instead focuses on how the Lord empowered him to preach the message regardless. While Paul did not feel abandoned by God, when abandoned by brothers or sisters in Christ, it can be easy to mistake that for abandonment by God. Often, I have heard people talk about someone failing them and then finish by saying, "I don't know what God is doing."

When all else and all others fail you, take heed of Jesus's intimate cry of "My God, my God . . ." and pray "Our Father in heaven." The "our" serving as a reminder that as you pray for yourself, you pray for others. Even those who should know better but have treated you unjustly or cruelly.

In such dark seasons, the prayer "Our Father in heaven" will be the means by which your preaching is marked by grace and not bitterness. This confidence rests on what God has achieved through the work of Christ on the cross. While there may be times when you feel like praying, "My God, my God, why have you forsaken me," if you do, add "Our Father in heaven."

For the promise of your Father to you is "Never will I leave you; never will I forsake you" (Deut 31:6; Heb 13:5). This promise is inescapable. The message is even the same if you say the verse backwards, "You forsake I will never; you leave I will never."

Such is our Father in heaven.

Reflection

Consider a time when you felt abandoned in your ministry. Listen to Jesus's cry from the cross for you.

Pray

Our Father in heaven.

10

Hallowed Be Your Name

A Prayer for Preachers Needing Courage

John 19:4–6, 12–15, 19–22

Once more Pilate came out and said to the Jews gathered there, "Look, I am bringing him out to you to let you know that I find no basis for a charge against him." When Jesus came out wearing the crown of thorns and the purple robe, Pilate said to them, "Here is the man!"

As soon as the chief priests and their officials saw him, they shouted, "Crucify! Crucify!"

Pilate tried to set Jesus free, but the Jewish leaders kept shouting, "If you let this man go, you are no friend of Caesar. Anyone who claims to be a king opposes Caesar."

When Pilate heard this, he brought Jesus out and sat down on the judge's seat at a place known as the Stone Pavement (which in Aramaic is Gabbatha). It was the day of Preparation of the Passover; it was about noon.

"Here is your king," Pilate said to the Jews.

But they shouted, "Take him away! Take him away! Crucify him!"

Pilate had a notice prepared and fastened to the cross. It read: Jesus of Nazareth, the King of the Jews. Many of the Jews read this sign, for the place where Jesus was crucified was near the city, and the sign was written in Aramaic, Latin and Greek. The chief priests of the Jews protested to Pilate, "Do not write 'The King of the Jews,' but that this man claimed to be king of the Jews."

Pilate answered, "What I have written, I have written."

Pontius Pilate was not a preacher. But, as brief as it is, the notice he had nailed to the cross is as close to a sermon by him as you are likely to find: "Jesus of Nazareth, the King of the Jews."

All four Gospels record the moments Jesus stands before the Roman governor. Yet only the Gospel of John details in depth the conversation Pilate shares with Jesus (John 18:28–19:16). Surrounding this conversation is the relentless noise of the Jewish leaders demanding Jesus's death and the crowd shouting, "Crucify! Crucify!" (John 19:6).

Pilate is torn.

He hears Jesus declare life: "Everyone on the side of truth listens to me" (John 18:37). He hears his own heart discern justice, "Look, I am bringing him out to you to let you know that I find no basis for a charge against him" (John 19:4). He hears the Jewish leaders and crowd demand death, "We have a law, and according to that law he must die, because he claimed to be the Son of God" (John 19:7).

Pilate is afraid.

He hears the Jews say Jesus claims to be the Son of God. And Jesus has already told Pilate that his kingdom is not of this world (John 18:36). He hears the Jews say if Pilate allows Jesus to live, then Pilate is no friend of Caesar (John 19:12).

Pilate is confronted with an earthly kingdom.

He hears Jesus say that any power Pilate has over Jesus is "given to [him] from above" (John 19:11).

Pilate is confronted with a heavenly kingdom.

The picture of Pilate in the Gospel of John is of a man in turmoil. Yet twice in the midst of the storm Pilate makes two statements about Christ. Both statements have a sense of stillness and significance about them. Both statements even have the sense of an appeal: as if the Jewish leaders and crowd are the judge and Pilate is appealing to them in the role of a defence lawyer.

Pilate's first appeal is "Here is the man!" (John 19:5).

At this point Jesus has been flogged, mocked and hit by the Roman soldiers. He is wearing a crown of thorns and is clothed in a purple robe. The King of Heaven taking the very nature of a servant: being found as a man (Phil 2:6–8). But the crowd deliver their judgement, "Crucify! Crucify!" (John 19:6).

Pilate's second appeal is "Here is your king" (John 19:14).

At this point Pilate sits on the judge's seat, and John records that it was the day of Preparation for the Passover. The King of Heaven taking the very nature of the Lamb of God: being found as a Saviour (John 1:29). Again, the crowd deliver their judgement: "Take him away! Take him away! Crucify him!" (John 19:15).

Pilate hands Jesus over to be crucified and makes his declaration: "Pilate had a notice prepared and fastened to the cross. It read, 'Jesus of Nazareth, the King of the Jews'" (John 19:19).

So, Pilate preaches.

Here is the man: Jesus of Nazareth.

Here is your king: The King of the Jews.

Hallowed be your name.

Pilate the preacher. Preaching in the main languages available to him: Aramaic, Latin and Greek. Preaching the name and title of Christ. Preaching a message that offended those who accused Jesus and worked so hard to have him sentenced to death: "The chief priests of the Jews protested to Pilate, "Do not write 'The King of the Jews,' but that this man claimed to be king of the Jews." Pilate answered, "What I have written, I have written" (John 19:21–22).

There it is: "What I have written, I have written." Finally, Pilate states a position from which he refuses to move. For, up until now, the picture of Pilate is one of a man who was swayed, manipulated and hassled into an action he knew to be unjust. Yes, Pilate was the Roman governor and had power. He was also someone who was very unpopular with the Jews.[1] He was a violent man who used force to suppress any sign of trouble from the Jewish community (e.g. Luke 13:1). He was ambitious and no doubt wanted to advance his political career. So, his actions and decisions were as much about protecting his reputation in the eyes of Rome as attending to local matters in Jerusalem. "Thus Pilate was not only cruel but, like many bullies, fearful of exposure to those in authority over him."[2] But up until now in John's gospel, the picture of Pilate is one of a man who acted against his conscience and what he knew to be right. The sign he fastened on the cross was a defiant tribute to this man who had clearly impacted Pilate. John describes that the silence of Jesus, as much as his words, amazed Pilate.

"Jesus of Nazareth, the King of the Jews." The sign seems to speak of Pilate's regret, remorse, reverence and sense of revelation. The sign – which angered others – seems personal to Pilate. The sign has the sense that Pilate reached his limit and finally made his declaration about who he believed Jesus to be. Pilate's experience reflects a pattern from earlier in the Gospel of John: people's status being stripped away in the presence of Jesus. .

---

1. Keener, *Commentary on the Gospel*, 665–667.
2. Keener, 667.

We see it in the story of Nicodemus, a Pharisee, who comes to Jesus under the cover of night (John 3:1–14). His status as one of Israel's teachers is stripped away and he encounters Jesus as the Son of Man.

We see it in the story of the Samaritan woman at the well (John 4:1–26). Her status as an outcast is stripped away and she encounters Jesus as the Messiah.

We see it in the story of the royal official who wanted Jesus to heal his dying son (John 4:43–54). His status as a royal official is stripped away, and towards the end of the story, he is simply described as a father. He encounters Jesus as the Word made flesh.

We see it in the story of Pilate. His status as governor is stripped away and he encounters Jesus as King.

Hallowed be your name.

Yet such a declaration, such a sermon, now seems too little too late. The words literally hang over the Person who did not deserve to die. This declaration communicates Pilate's shame. While it is a sign declaring the truth of the Crucified One, it is also a sign declaring the failure of someone who proved too weak in the presence of evil. He declared, "Here is the man! Here is your king," but the cries of "Crucify!" drowned out his declaration.

Yes, we know that in the sovereignty of God, the crucifixion of Jesus was the plan of redemption. Yet, in the unfolding of that plan we see the failure and frailty of humans to act with courage and justice. We see the bitterness of regret and remorse. We see it in the distress of Peter, the despair of Judas, the disappearance of the disciples and the display of Pilate.

There are those times when we are too silent, for too long, about too much. Those times when we have failed to honour the name of Christ. Those times when our words and actions do not pray "Hallowed be your name." Those times when events overtake us, and we are left with the feeling that we did not do all we could when we should. Now, our words – our sermons – seem flat and hollow. They seem to have lost their timing and therefore their power. Whereas, if we had spoken up in the midst of turmoil, perhaps our words might have been prophetic; but now they seem pathetic.

Now, like Pilate, it seems the best we can do is place a sign on the cross. A statement that represents what we wished we had had the strength to have said before things had got to this stage.

It feels like a failure. It feels too late.

It does not feel like my sermon declares "Hallowed be your name."

Yet, regardless of what others might say to us by way of criticism or condemnation, we at least can say with Pilate, "What I have written, I have written." A statement that is delayed but is nevertheless defiant.

"What I have preached, I have preached. Even though you might have grounds to criticise me – I preach from a place of weakness that still declares 'Jesus of Nazareth, the King of the Jews.' My failure and weakness do not make such a statement any less true. And so my preaching prays: Hallowed be your name."

Pilate's message was in the major languages of his day: Aramaic, Latin and Greek. His was the last word even though it was a word that was late. Our message is also in the major languages of our day: the languages of heart, mind, soul and strength. There may be times when our message is late – but it still seeks to declare "Hallowed be your name."

When I was in my early twenties, I worked for a government department. I was the only Christian in an office of about ten workers. Some of my office colleagues were retired from the army. They were veterans who had seen combat in places such as Malaysia (in the 1950s) and Vietnam (in the 1960s/1970s). They were hard men. They did not believe in Christ and would often use the Lord's name in vain as they swore in conversation. One day, after one of them again had used the Lord's name in this way, I said, "For someone who doesn't believe in God, you sure do pray a lot!" That was the last time I ever heard them speak in such a way. Somehow my comment won their respect.

Yet, a couple of years later, I once asked one of my colleagues (not one of the army veterans), "What is it about my faith in Christ that appeals to you; and what is it that repels you?" She answered, "What appeals is that you are here. I once worked with a Jehovah Witness, and they would never join in any activities when we socialized. But you do. That appeals to me. But what repels me is your silence. There are times when injustice happens and as a Christian I expect you to speak up. But you don't. You stay silent. That repels me from Christianity." She was right. Her words reminded me of an earlier challenge she had made to me a few months before. It happened one day after I returned to work after lunch. During the lunch break, I had an encounter with a person who I met for the first and only time. I related the encounter to my work colleague. I said, "He was so racist. He was saying all kinds of things." She replied, "And I guarantee you did not say a word to challenge him." To my shame, she was right. My silence in the presence of injustice did not display the kind of Christianity that interested her.

I realized then that there was something of Pilate in me. That in the presence of hostility, or the threat of saying something that was necessary but unpopular, I remained silent. As someone who bears the name "Christian," such silence does not communicate "Hallowed be your name." Such silence and inactivity weaken the integrity of the person who is a preacher. It takes more courage to say challenging things person to person than it does to say such things from the pulpit. It takes more courage to hallow and honour the name of Christ one on one than it does from the safety of the pulpit.

The image of Pilate's sign on the cross of Christ is an unlikely source of encouragement for those of us who have failed in our courage as preachers. As described earlier, Pilate's sign speaks of regret, remorse, reverence and revelation. His sign, "Jesus of Nazareth, the King of the Jews," is a public statement that emerges from a personal failure. That the sign is nailed to the cross is a statement in itself. Part of Colossians 2 puts it like this:

> When you were dead in your sins and in the uncircumcision of your flesh, God made you alive with Christ. He forgave us all our sins, having canceled the charge of our legal indebtedness, which stood against us and condemned us; he has taken it away, nailing it to the cross. And having disarmed the powers and authorities, he made a public spectacle of them, triumphing over them by the cross. (Col 2:13–15)

The cross by which we are alive with Christ, by which that which condemns and haunts us is taken away and disempowered, by which we can know triumph in and through Christ. So, even in those times when we have been too silent for too long, and spoken too late, the cross provides a way for us to still pray and preach "Hallowed be your name."

Reflection

Think of a time when you were too silent, for too long, about too much. If you fastened a sign on the cross, what would it say?

Pray

Hallowed be your name.

11

Your Kingdom Come
A Prayer for Preachers Needing Hope

Luke 23:35–43

The people stood watching, and the rulers even sneered at him. They said, "He saved others; let him save himself if he is God's Messiah, the Chosen One."

The soldiers also came up and mocked him. They offered him wine vinegar and said, "If you are the king of the Jews, save yourself."

There was a written notice above him, which read: THIS IS THE KING OF THE JEWS.

One of the criminals who hung there hurled insults at him: "Aren't you the Messiah? Save yourself and us!"

But the other criminal rebuked him. "Don't you fear God," he said, "since you are under the same sentence? We are punished justly, for we are getting what our deeds deserve. But this man has done nothing wrong."

Then he said, "Jesus, remember me when you come into your kingdom."

Jesus answered him, "Truly I tell you, today you will be with me in paradise."

Despair is frightening.

Despair is fueled by the experience of being alone and isolated. Few, if any, are aware of the dark fortress that slowly builds, stone by stone, in your heart and mind. Few, if any, can penetrate the dark fortress that imprisons you.

If you are struggling with feelings of despair and are in public ministry, such as preaching, this can increase the sense of despair. You speak the word of God while desperately needing to hear the word of God. You give but need to receive. You speak but need to be heard. You fill others, but you are empty. You are increasingly scared that someone will notice. You are increasingly scared that you will be found out. You are increasingly scared that you will not survive.

As a preacher, you are limited in who you can confide in, and your current despair is hardly material for a sermon illustration. To speak of it publicly while in the midst of it could cause harm for others. Perhaps you can refer to it at a later time when you preach. But you need to be on the other side of despair. You have a pastoral responsibility to be wise in what you say and when you say it. There is a difference between displaying vulnerability as a preacher and dumping vulnerability on the people. To put it another way, we can either testify how Christ's power is made perfect in our weakness and leave people with the vision of God's grace, or we can testify how our weakness leaves us powerless and leave people with the vision of our grief. Also, people tend to remember you by the last thing you say and may not be present when you report new life and light. So, there is a need to protect yourself during such a time.

I once attended a panel discussion for preachers and pastors. One new pastor spoke of the emotional pain she experienced in ministry and asked how best to cope with this in the midst of preaching. It was this new pastor's practice to include descriptions of her pain when preaching. She not only cried telling us the story but said she cried when preaching and describing her pain. I could not see how she could have a lasting preaching ministry by using the pulpit to regularly express her anguish. As a preacher, appropriate ways to have emotional needs met away from the pulpit need to be found.

Along with this is the temptation to stay silent anyway. As someone in a leadership role, to admit you are in despair evokes a sense of shame. You think, "Leaders shouldn't feel this way, much less preachers!" So the isolation grows as does the fortress. The darkness deepens and any way of escape fades from view.

Despair is frightening.

I have spoken with pastors who have been in this kind of space. Nothing seems to be going right and all that is wrong feels like it is their fault. They still sense God's call, but they do not sense God's empowerment. They know things cannot continue as they are, and they fear an approaching end is nearing. Things are happening and they cannot stop it, let alone understand it.

Despair is frightening.

The forces which drive a person to despair are many. The exchange between Jesus and the two criminals on the cross provide a striking picture of despair

(Luke 23:35–43). All three are dying. The air is full of mocking and taunting. The insults come from three directions and are directed at Jesus alone. First, the rulers recall Jesus's ministry and speak out of anger: "He saved others; let him save himself if he is God's Messiah, the Chosen One" (Luke 23:35). Second, the soldiers refer to Pilate's written notice on the cross and speak out of ignorance: "If you are the king of the Jews, save yourself" (Luke 23:37). Third, one of the criminals rages about Jesus's claims and speaks out of bitterness: "Aren't you the Messiah? Save yourself and us!" (Luke 23:39).

To put it another way, the rulers mock Jesus out of anger for what he has done; the soldiers out of ignorance for what others say he has done; and the criminal out of bitterness for what Jesus hasn't done. It is unsurprising that the rulers and soldiers mock and insult Jesus in this way. However, it is a dark image of despair that one of the criminals joins in. He is dying in the company of the Saviour yet sides with those tormenting Jesus. He echoes Jesus's tormentors' words and blasphemes. His last reserves of strength are used to speak words of anger and bitterness. Death and despair are drowning this criminal in every way. As such, his despairing death is deeply tragic. For within reach from his darkness is the Light of the World, just a prayer away. But it is a prayer he never prays.

Your kingdom come.

We probably cannot imagine ever plunging to such depths of despair as represented by this particular criminal. However, if despair takes hold of your heart and is allowed to grow unchallenged, you will be surprised at what you hear yourself saying. When confronted by extreme moments in life when God does not seem present, I have heard strong Christians despair and say shocking things. In such times, despair can grow, and faith can fade. It is as if the accusations from this incident at the cross are repeated. Despairing disciples angrily and unjustly state what God has done, what they have heard he has done, and what he should have done.

But there is a second criminal in this story. His life, too, is being brutally extinguished. His situation is like the other criminal in every way. He, too, has committed a crime worthy of death, and there is no one to save him. There is no mercy for him. He, too, is confronted with despair, and he, too, hears the insults being shouted at Jesus. But unlike the other criminal, he speaks a diffcrent word. Unlike the other criminal, he disrupts his despair.

Your kingdom come.

"But the other criminal rebuked him. 'Don't you fear God,' he said, 'since you are under the same sentence? We are punished justly, for we are getting what our deeds deserve. But this man has done nothing wrong.' Then he said,

'Jesus, remember me when you come into your kingdom'" (Luke 23:40–42). This criminal does not add his voice to the anger about what Jesus had done, or to the ignorance about what Jesus might have done, or to the bitterness about what Jesus is not doing. Instead, he appeals to Jesus about what he *can* do.

This criminal gave voice to hope from the place of despair, entrusting himself to Christ: "Jesus, remember me when you come into your kingdom" (Luke 23:42).

"Remember me."

The criminal prays a form of "Your kingdom come" but expects that it can only be at a later time. I suspect we would have the same expectation. "Your kingdom come – but I don't see it now in my distress and despair. But remember me. When you come into the fullness of your kingdom." I imagine anyone in despair might get to the point when they think they have said their last prayer. They might think they do not have the strength left to continue to preach any longer. So, they pray into the darkness. Hoping that somehow their prayer will be heard, even if their ministry does not survive to see the fruit of that. Such prayers feel like the end of the matter. Not the solution – the end.

Your kingdom come.

The criminal sees the present as finalized ("We are punished justly"); the past as irredeemable ("For we are getting what our deeds deserve"); and the future as in God's hands ("Remember me").

If the criminal's words disrupted his despair, Jesus's words destroy it: "Truly I tell you, today you will be with me in paradise" (Luke 23:43). These words are intensely personal. In the Gospels the phrase "truly I tell you" occurs many times. However, only Jesus ever begins a statement with this phrase. In doing so, he ensures we understand the certainty of what he is saying. Further, the only time Jesus addresses the phrase "truly I tell you" to a single person is to the criminal here in Luke 23.[1] Every other time it is directed to a gathering of people. But this time it is one to one.

The criminal despairing of life has been heard, and Jesus's words are for him alone in that moment.

Your kingdom come.

The beauty of Jesus's promise is found in one word: "Today." In Jewish faith, paradise is thought of in terms of time rather than place.[2] Paradise is a time which is the ultimate Sabbath rest, centred on the Messiah. Jesus's reply has an excess of meaning: "Today you will be with me in paradise." The time

---
1. Harris, *Seven Sayings*, 38.
2. Robinson, *Essential Judaism*, 88.

and place that is paradise is centred on himself. The criminal literally joined Jesus in death and in paradise.

In 1 Peter, we read words which illustrate Jesus's example on the cross and the kind of hope the criminal enjoyed:

> To this you were called, because Christ suffered for you, leaving you an example, that you should follow in his steps.
>
> "He committed no sin,
> and no deceit was found in his mouth."
>
> When they hurled their insults at him, he did not retaliate; when he suffered, he made no threats. Instead, he entrusted himself to him who judges justly.
>
> "He himself bore our sins" in his body on the cross, so that we might die to sins and live for righteousness; "by his wounds you have been healed." For "you were like sheep going astray," but now you have returned to the Shepherd and Overseer of your souls. (1 Pet 2:21–25)

In reflecting on this incident on the cross, one biblical scholar draws out a beautiful challenge for us: "As we look at our Saviour hanging on the cross and refusing to retaliate, we must open our hearts to allow the same 'powerlessness' to affect every aspect of our lives. When we surrender power over our lives to live for God and others, our souls will be imbued with the power and mystery of 'Christ in you, the hope of glory' (Col 1:27)."[3]

Your kingdom come.

But what of you? What of your despair? Our prayer for this reflection is "Your kingdom come." In the tradition of the criminal, our prayer is infused with the hope that Jesus will "Remember me." For someone in despair the petition to "Remember me" holds so much.

In Melbourne, Australia, there is a Jewish Holocaust centre. The centre is a museum and place of education telling the story of the Holocaust in World War 2.[4] Off to one side in the museum is a very small room called the Memorial

---

3. Takatemjen, *Luke*, 1383.

4. The Holocaust is the name given to describe Adolf Hitler and the Nazi party's genocide of the Jewish community in Germany and Europe, beginning in the 1930s and taking place, especially, during the period of World War 2 (1939–1945). Hitler and the Nazis called this the "Final Solution." Concentration camps were built throughout Germany and the countries they occupied. No one was spared, as young, old, male and female Jews were herded into cattle cars on trains and transported from all over Europe to these death camps. The most infamous of the camps was Auschwitz-Birkenau in Poland. Of the six million Jews killed in the camps, one

Room. On the wall is an account written by a woman called Eva. The account explains why the room exists. It begins, "Nobody really knew his name. He sat on the brick oven that spanned almost the entire length of the barracks. All day he swayed to and fro, no sound, no word came out of his mouth." What follows is a description of a traumatized nine-year-old boy, alone in Auschwitz-Birkenau. Eva herself is about thirteen years old at the time. One day the boy is suddenly jerked from his isolated, traumatized silence. Eva's story continues, "In great haste, he raced towards me, tears streaming down his face, his dark piercing brown eyes staring into mine and pleading, 'Eva, my name is Shmuel, I am nine years old, my turn has come, promise that you will say Kaddish [the Jewish prayer for the dead] after me, remember this day, this date, my name Shmuel!'" Eva recounts her panic. She did not know the day or date. But then she felt the tattooed number on her arm that all camp victims received. She told Shmuel that her tattooed number would be his Kaddish. "He walked away content, knowing that he will be remembered, with faith in God until the end." The story ends with Eva saying that with the dedication of the room, the burden has lifted. This small boy is remembered along with so many others who, in the words of Eva, "Whispered with their last breath Kaddish." And in this tiny room the walls are lined with name after name. All of them are remembered.

The existence of this room speaks of the human need to be seen and heard. It speaks of the human need to be remembered. Most of all by God.

When in despair, perhaps the most you can hope for is that sometime in the future God's kingdom will come and heal what little you have left. Your prayer for "Your kingdom come" has changed to "Remember me when you come into your kingdom." A prayer of faith for a later time but not for this time. Too much has happened and too little is left. When in despair, we can miss discerning, let alone expecting, the nearness of Christ. The immediacy of Christ. In response to your cry, Jesus is saying, "Today."

"When God 'remembers,' he does not just *think about* us. He *acts for* us, with power to save."[5]

Your kingdom come.

"Truly I tell you – you who are reading this – Today you will be with me."

---

million were killed in Auschwitz-Birkenau alone. The Jews were gassed to death in gas chambers. And many also died of starvation, disease and being worked to death as slave labour.

5. Rutledge, *Seven Last Words*, 20. Emphasis in original.

Reflection

Direct your thoughts to anything that causes you despair; and direct your thoughts to God who remembers you and acts for you.

Pray

Your kingdom come.

12

Your Will Be Done on Earth as It Is in Heaven
A Prayer for Preachers Needing Family

John 19:25–27

> Near the cross of Jesus stood his mother, his mother's sister, Mary the wife of Clopas, and Mary Magdalene. When Jesus saw his mother there, and the disciple whom he loved standing nearby, he said to her, "Woman, here is your son," and to the disciple, "Here is your mother." From that time on, this disciple took her into his home.

When I studied my theology qualification, my New Testament lecturer used to say that crucifixion was so horrific that ancient writers found it too awful to write about. The gospel accounts are the most detailed we have. Within that detail, across the four gospels, we read of the different people witnessing this dreadful event. Yet, of all the people present at the crucifixion, Jesus's mother is in a category of her own. A mother's love for her child cannot be exaggerated and the impact on a mother of witnessing the horror of her son being crucified escapes description. Simeon's prophecy when the infant Jesus was presented at the temple is one of the closest descriptions we have: "Then Simeon blessed them and said to Mary, his mother: 'This child is destined to cause the falling and rising of many in Israel, and to be a sign that will be spoken against, so that the thoughts of many hearts will be revealed. And a sword will pierce your own soul too'" (Luke 2:34–35).

"And a sword will pierce your own soul too." Scripture records that Mary was in the habit of pondering and treasuring things in her heart (Luke 2:19,

51). These words would have found their place in her heart waiting for the day of fulfilment.

Adding to the uniqueness of her place at the crucifixion are the words, "Near the cross of Jesus stood his mother . . ." (John 19:25). The phrase "cross of Jesus" only appears here in John's account. It somehow conveys a deeply personal element which is further deepened by the words "stood his mother." While the position of others are similarly described, Jesus's mother is mentioned first, which has the effect of further communicating a private pain that only a mother can know. Other women stand with her, but this mother's pain is hers alone.

Jesus sees her standing there, near John, "the disciple whom he loved." Of the seven words from the cross, the words he speaks to these two are the most tender and personal. They are words of compassion and care: "Woman, here is your son"; and "Here is your mother." The words highlight the situation of Jesus's mother – while clearly she is standing with others at the cross, there is an aloneness about her. She is isolated. Jesus's words give expression to Psalm 68:5–6:

> A father to the fatherless, a defender of widows,
> is God in his holy dwelling.
> God sets the lonely in families.

Your will be done on earth as it is in heaven.
Both literally and symbolically, the cross of Jesus is a source of care for the one who is deeply pained and alone. For the one who is lonely and isolated, hear the words of Jesus which show he sees your situation.

The ministry of preaching can unexpectedly be a lonely one. Here is a ministry which is always relating to groups of people. Whenever we preach, we do so in a community. Even during sermon preparation, the people we will be preaching to are in our hearts and minds. We have in mind how to best write the sermon for those who will hear it. We think of the people and what explanations are needed, what illustrations will be helpful and what applications will be necessary. Yet, preaching can still generate deep loneliness within the preacher.

For all the connection you enjoy with the congregation, there is also a point of separation. For you alone have wrestled with the Scripture you are preaching from and in that there is an aloneness. Regardless of how well you preach, parts remain which were either unsaid or not communicated to your satisfaction. You alone know the prayers you prayed and the fruit you hoped for. After the sermon, feedback and response can range from too much to not enough; from deeply encouraging to harshly critical; from exciting to depressing.

After one sermon, which I thought I had preached well, someone immediately approached me. The speed with which they walked towards me caused me to think they needed to talk about something important from the sermon. However, all they wanted to know was how to fix one of their electronic devices. On another occasion – again, after I thought the sermon had gone well – one of the first people to comment pointed out that one of my biblical references was off by one number. There was no engagement with the rest of the sermon. Still another rejoined the Mormon church as a result of one of my sermons! Preaching can be lonely.

Your will be done on earth as it is in heaven.

By way of illustration, the story of Jacob in Genesis 32:22–32 helps as a way of thinking about it. Jacob is heading towards an encounter with his brother Esau, and he is afraid. Jacob sends all his family and possessions ahead of him, and he remains alone. Then a man wrestles with Jacob all night. We learn at the end of the story that the "man" was God. There is a lot of mystery in the story. But this image of Jacob wrestling with God, being blessed with a new name (which represents new character) and limping away from the encounter sums up what a preaching ministry can be like. You are alone with God, and while there are others involved, the wrestling involves only you. The image of night adds to the sense of aloneness. At one level, as you prepare a sermon, you are reenacting Genesis 32. Others will benefit from the fight, but you alone as preacher must wrestle with God. You alone limp away from the encounter, and you alone know the change in your character as a result. Preaching can be lonely.

Your will be done on earth as it is in heaven.

The words from John 19:25 describe your place: "Near the cross of Jesus stood [you]." Your soul hungers for words of compassion and care which relieve your loneliness. You long to hear words in the tradition of what Jesus said to his mother and disciple; words which join people together.

My wife and I had the privilege of being in another country for a couple of months so I could work on a preaching project. I had high expectations about what I could achieve during that time. However, when I arrived and began my work, it was as if I had lost my ability to think and engage with preaching issues. Every day was a battle. While there were times of encouragement from God and the Scriptures, there were lots of times of discouragement when I could not produce much. And what I did produce seemed poor. Overall I felt like I was declining rather than growing. Indeed, in my journal I wrote that I wondered if I was losing my preaching gift. Things felt like they were ending. I was alone in it, and I could not stop the increase of despair and loneliness in my life. I was scared. It was as if I was standing near the cross of Jesus and overwhelmed by death. The future was slipping away.

Next door to the little cottage where we were staying were other overseas visitors: an American pastor and his wife. They were on a period of leave from their church. The pastor's name was Steve. On occasions, Steve and I would be talking about something general. Then, in the conversation, and without warning, Steve would startle me with a statement. His statement was directed at me and was personal, strong, specific, stirring, encouraging and warm. He would make an observation about my writing or teaching and call me to expand and continue in my writing and teaching. I was totally surprised by his comments. I asked why he said what he said, because I could not see any connection with what we were talking about. But what he was doing was listening to the music, the heart, behind my words. Music, or a heart, that I could no longer hear. Perhaps it was no accident that Steve was an outstanding musician and songwriter. That was what Steve was doing, but I realized there was Someone else doing something. Jesus was saying to me in my aloneness, "Here is your brother," and my brother took me in.

When we were about to return to our home countries, Steve gave me and my wife a gift. It was a piece of beautiful folk art he must have spent hours creating. The craft is called "scherenschnitte," which means "scissor cutting." The craft came from eighteenth-century German immigrants to his home state of Pennsylvania (USA). The artwork was a delicate cutting in paper with fine detail in the shape of a heart. Within the heart, there were tiny flowers and branches and two winged birds with a smaller heart between them. On the back of this treasured gift Steve wrote an explanation:

> The large heart is the love of God embracing and surrounding the two of you as the winged birds. Your love for each other, and Christ and his calling, are symbolized by the smaller and united heart within the larger heart. And the flowers represent the fruit God has prepared beforehand for the two of you to bear. And know that somewhere there is another couple praying for you.

Your will be done on earth as it is in heaven.

There are times when we come to a place when we have little strength to do much more. In our weakened state, loneliness and isolation sap our strength and hope. The task of preaching becomes more difficult. In such times, may the echo of this word from the cross provide for you the friendship and new family that you need. May you experience the care and compassion of Christ through the kindness and thoughtfulness of others. For God sets the lonely in families and seeks to build a community in his name. He wants you to be cared for and your sense of aloneness to melt away.

For, insofar as this happens, "Your will be done on earth as it is in heaven."

Reflection

As a preacher, do you experience loneliness? Or have you recognized loneliness in a fellow preacher? In what ways is God inviting you into a family or asking you to be a family for someone?

Pray

Your will be done on earth as it is in heaven.

13

Give Us Today Our Daily Bread
A Prayer for Preachers Needing Nourishment

John 19:28–29

Later, knowing that everything had now been finished, and so that Scripture would be fulfilled, Jesus said, "I am thirsty." A jar of wine vinegar was there, so they soaked a sponge in it, put the sponge on a stalk of the hyssop plant, and lifted it to Jesus's lips.

Of the seven sayings of Jesus from the cross, "I am thirsty" is possibly the one we can relate to easiest. Everyone experiences thirst so we know something of what it means to be thirsty. The words, "I am thirsty," have a point of connection with our human experience. However, there is a major point of difference. We don't know the kind of thirst experienced after being on trial all night, being flogged by Roman soldiers, carrying a cross, being nailed to it and hanging on it for hours.

Jesus's simple yet agonizing statement both connects with our human condition and goes beyond it in unimaginable torture. "I am thirsty" names a basic human need and speaks a divine word in response. "I am thirsty" is spoken by the One whose life is poured out so that we can know fullness.

John's description of this word from the cross is preceded by the comment, "So that Scripture would be fulfilled, Jesus said . . ." (John 19:28). John does not give details of which Scripture is fulfilled. However, it's as if verses from afar have foreseen this moment on the cross and pay homage.[1] It's as if these

---

[1]. The phrase "verse from afar" is used to describe a particular kind of sermon Jewish Hasidic rabbis preached in the Medieval Age. These rabbis would read a text from the Bible and, without commenting on it, would go to an entirely different Bible verse from afar. They would pose a problem or issue from this second verse and then seek to provide the solution from the original verse. Kunst, *Burning Word*, 64–66.

verses from afar describe a deep and unfulfilled need and now find fulfilment in this cry from the cross. Such verses from afar might include:

> I am poured out like water,
> and all my bones are out of joint.
> My heart has turned to wax;
> it has melted within me.
> My mouth is dried up like a potsherd,
> and my tongue sticks to the roof of my mouth;
> you lay me in the dust of death. (Ps 22:14–15)

> I am worn out calling for help;
> my throat is parched.
> My eyes fail,
> looking for my God.

> They put gall in my food
> and gave me vinegar for my thirst. (Ps 69:3, 21)

Other verses from afar are closer to the words, "I am thirsty," given they are also in the Gospel of John. It is as if these verses speak of the gift of God yet point to the cost by which this gift comes. Mysteriously, somehow the words on the cross fulfil what Jesus has promised previously in the Gospel of John.

The one who cries out, "I am thirsty," is the one who used water to create the superb wine for a wedding (John 2:1–11).

The one who cries out, "I am thirsty," is the one who asked a Samaritan woman for a drink (John 4:7). She is shocked that a Jew would ask her, a Samaritan woman, for a drink. Jews and Samaritans did not associate. But Jesus responds, "If you knew the gift of God and who it is that asks you for a drink, you would have asked him and he would have given you living water" (John 4:10).

The one who cries out, "I am thirsty," is the one who stood up on the last and greatest day of the Feast of Tabernacles and said in a loud voice, "Let anyone who is thirsty come to me and drink. Whoever believes in me, as Scripture has said, rivers of living water will flow from within them" (John 7:37–38).

Elsewhere in the Gospels, other verses from afar foreshadow the cry "I am thirsty."

The one who cries out, "I am thirsty," is the one who took a cup at the Last Supper, the symbol of his blood shed on the cross, and offered it to his disciples to drink (Matt 26:27–29). He adds that he will not drink from the fruit of the vine until the day when he drinks it anew with his disciples in his

Father's kingdom. The words, "I am thirsty," and the attempt by those at the cross to offer him wine vinegar (John 19:29) emphasize Jesus's thirst and point to an ultimate fulfilment.

The one who cries out, "I am thirsty," had earlier prayed in the garden of Gethsemane, "My Father, if it is not possible for this cup to be taken away unless I drink it, may your will be done" (Matt 26:42). Jesus drinks the cup and experiences a dying thirst.

"So that Scripture would be fulfilled, Jesus said, 'I am thirsty.'"

As preachers, we, too, cry from afar and find fulfilment in these words of Jesus. Our cry from afar is from a place of depletion. Preaching is costly. To preach the word of God is life-giving in more than one sense. We gain life from the privilege of such a ministry; we give life to others as we preach the Scriptures; and yet we also expend life as we do so. Preaching can be exhausting.

After one sermon I preached, and at the end of the worship service, a woman said to me, "I am sure you are glad you gave birth to that sermon." She was right. The sermon had been burdening me, and it took life from me to preach it. Somehow, she recognized the toll the sermon had taken, and perhaps as only a woman can, she used the imagery of childbirth. I guess it is no accident that we talk about "delivering a sermon."

As preachers, we can find ourselves depleted. Our reserves are low, and yet the next sermon needs to be written. For those in a regular preaching ministry, the demands can be relentless. Also, in your leadership position as a preacher, there will be times when you are misheard or misunderstood. Both within and out of the pulpit. There will be times when you are not in a position to defend yourself or explain yourself. Or times when you could say something in your defence, but wisdom prevails, and it is better to stay silent. One of the best pieces of ministry advice I ever received was from a church elder. We were dealing with a difficult pastoral situation as a leadership, and we were receiving criticism from some members of the church. I said to the elder, "But if we told them what really was happening then maybe they would understand." She replied, "Leaders do not always get to tell their story." She was right even though there is a cost attached to not telling your story.

Over time, preachers can find themselves in a spiritual place which is increasingly the kind of place Psalm 63 describes:

> You, God, are my God,
> earnestly I seek you;
> I thirst for you,
> my whole being longs for you,

in a dry and parched land
where there is no water. (Ps 63:1)

We thirst. Our ministry and our whole being is as a dry and parched land where there is no water. What to do?

So that Scripture would be fulfilled, and our longing filled, we, too, cry from afar. Our verse from afar directed to the cross is "Give us today our daily bread." How is our prayer for daily bread met in this cry from the cross about thirst? The one who cried out on the cross, "I am thirsty," had earlier in his ministry spoken of hunger and thirst in the same breath. Jesus identified himself as the Bread of Life who satisfies hunger and quenches thirst. Jesus said, "I am the bread of life. Whoever comes to me will never go hungry, and whoever believes in me will never be thirsty" (John 6:35). Our deep hunger and thirst is promised to be met in Christ. Our cry, "Give us today our daily bread," is fulfilled at the cost of the Bread of Life saying, "I am thirsty." Jesus's life is poured out like a drink offering, and we are filled.

Give us today our daily bread.

How this happens often escapes explanation. There is no magical formula – it is the grace and gift of God. He has the means to provide you with the nourishment you need in ways which leave you in no doubt that God has intervened.

When I was pastoring, I was in a meeting in which I was verbally attacked by another pastor. I had never met this pastor before, but he was yelling and insulting me about a decision he disagreed with. For my own safety, I left the meeting. I felt utterly emptied by the attack. I walked outside, and instead of returning to the church, I turned and walked in the opposite direction. In my depleted and wounded state, I decided to go and visit my mentor. He was one of the best preachers I have known. He was a man with a gentle spirit and a deep love and knowledge of the Scriptures. However, he was now well-advanced in years and, due to a series of strokes, could no longer speak. I arrived at his place and sat with him. Without mentioning what had just happened, I talked to him even though he could not reply. But he smiled at me and there was light in his eyes. Eventually, I said that I would like to pray for him, and I took his hand and began to pray. But it was as if I had taken the hand of Christ. As I prayed for him, I experienced deep healing for my bruised spirit. Life seemed to flow from him to me even though he could not say a word. I left his presence whole again.

Give us today our daily bread.

Maybe what I had experienced was the ministry of someone who was imitating the ministry of Jesus: pouring himself out so that others could be sustained. God can provide our daily bread in a parched land through the ministry of such people. We see this in the relationship between Paul and Timothy, whereby Paul is being poured out and, even so, sustains the younger pastor Timothy: "But you, keep your head in all situations, endure hardship, do the work of an evangelist, discharge all the duties of your ministry. For I am already being poured out like a drink offering, and the time for my departure is near. I have fought the good fight, I have finished the race, I have kept the faith" (2 Tim 4:5–7).

"I am thirsty."
Give us today our daily bread.
Take and drink. Take and eat.

Reflection

List the ways you feel depleted.

Pray

Give us today our daily bread.

14

Forgive Us Our Debts as We Also Have Forgiven Our Debtors
A Prayer for Preachers Needing Release

Luke 23:32–34

Two other men, both criminals, were also led out with him to be executed. When they came to the place called the Skull, they crucified him there, along with the criminals – one on his right, the other on his left. Jesus said, "Father, forgive them, for they do not know what they are doing." And they divided up his clothes by casting lots.

Perhaps, of the seven cries from the cross, this one is the most challenging. This description of the crucifixion shows that, in contrast to the magnitude of the injustice Jesus suffered, his capacity for forgiveness was greater. We see the nature of God: "But where sin increased, grace increased all the more" (Rom 5:20).

In just a few words, Luke sets the scene before us. He does so by stating one fact after another which, together, build a dark picture of terrible injustice. Each statement has the force of a hammer blow driving a nail of injustice into the flesh of Jesus.

He states that two others were led out with Jesus. They are named as criminals, which communicates that Jesus is being treated as one too. They are going to be executed, the worst fate for criminals. The name of the place of execution deepens the darkness: the Skull. The criminals are crucified on Jesus's right and left. This echoes the practice of seating those being honoured on either side of a king, but here it has a mocking quality about it. The king between the two criminals wears a cruel crown, and his throne is an instrument of torture.[1] Unlike in infancy, when royalty bowed before him, worshipped him and offered gifts of gold, frankincense and myrrh (Matt 2:11), those before him now divide up his few earthly possessions.

The injustice is enormous but the forgiveness more so.

"Father, forgive them, for they do not know what they are doing." The love shown is extraordinary. Jesus addresses his Father by name. This is one of three times on the cross when Jesus addresses his Father in such an intimate way. The other two occasions are when Jesus cries, "My God, my God, why have you forsaken me?" (Matt 27:46; Mark 15:34) and "Father, into your hands I commit my spirit" (Luke 23:46). These other two occasions are at the end of three hours of darkness which covered the land and just before Jesus breathed his last. From within deep darkness, Jesus calls his Father by name. That Jesus asks his Father by name to forgive highlights the complete darkness and death that is humanity's in a world devoid of God's forgiveness.

The depth of love and grace is seen further in that Jesus makes his request even though there is no confession or repentance evident from those crucifying him. Scripture explains this mystery best: "But God demonstrates his own love for us in this: While we were still sinners, Christ died for us (Rom 5:8)"; "This is love: not that we loved God, but that he loved us and sent his Son as an atoning sacrifice for our sins" (1 John 4:10).

This is not to suggest that we are excused from the disciplines of confession and repentance before God, but it does suggest an attitude to adopt when forgiving others. Rather than withholding forgiveness from others until they confess their sin against us and repent, are we prepared to forgive from our heart in the absence of these?

Forgive us our debts, as we also have forgiven our debtors.

The parable of the Unmerciful Servant (Matt 18:21–34) explores this issue after Peter asks how many times he needs to forgive someone. The point of the parable is the contrast between the king's forgiveness of a servant's huge debt, only for that same servant to refuse to forgive a tiny debt owed him by a fellow servant. John Stott wrote, "Once our eyes have been opened to see the enormity of our offence against God, the injuries which others have done to us appear by comparison extremely trifling. If, on the other hand, we have an exaggerated view of the offense of others, it proves that we have minimized

---

1. The Gospel of Luke does not mention the crown of thorns, but of course we know of its existence from the other gospel accounts (Matt 27:28–29; Mark 15:17; John 19:2).

our own."² The majesty of Jesus's cry from the cross shows the vastness of God's grace which can empower us to offer grace to others.

Forgive us our debts, as we also have forgiven our debtors.

Jesus's words from the cross provide us with the opportunity to pause and consider our lives and ministry as preachers. For, as preachers, we can ill afford to harbour unforgiveness in our hearts and expect to preach the gospel with integrity and freedom. As those who open the Scriptures for others, we have a greater responsibility to be an example of how to live according to the Scriptures. Without forgiveness, there is no Christian faith. Forgiveness is the lifeblood of a community and of the individuals who make up that community.

Forgive us our debts, as we also have forgiven our debtors.

In considering the place and need for forgiveness in your life as a preacher, consider these observations and examples.

Forgiveness is hard. That must be acknowledged. The journey to forgiveness can be complex and painful. Often, there is no easy way to do it. In addition to this, the painful memory of an offence can come to mind for no apparent reason. Just when we think we have forgiven someone, we feel like we still hold onto the offence. Be assured, such memories are a normal part of being human. Over time, they become less common and vivid. It is like pouring water over an open fire. The fire goes out, but if you move the ashes around, you will still find hot embers. Eventually they cool, but initially they can still cause pain. Yet we must guard against stoking the fire and fanning it into angry flames again. We might be the one who gets burnt.

Forgive us our debts, as we also have forgiven our debtors.

Who might you need to forgive? Or alternatively, who might you need to seek forgiveness from? I remember holding onto deep offence against my family for years. Then I became a Christian and found that my expectation that they needed to say sorry to me was replaced by the revelation that I first needed to say sorry to them. I had been holding onto the harm they had caused me but had been blind to the harm I had caused them. I was the one needing to ask for forgiveness; not them. I also realized I needed God's forgiveness for my offense against my family. When I experienced that forgiveness, I felt as if a concrete block had been removed from within me.

Forgive us our debts, as we also have forgiven our debtors.

In our house we have a striking example of the power of unforgiveness. For a wedding present, a woman gave us a beautiful painting of mountains and sea. We learned later that she had painted it herself. We also learned that

---

2. Stott, *Sermon on the Mount*, 91.

she had suffered for many years with a crippling disease in her hands. Her hands were unable to open and close normally. She could not hold things and needed special instruments to use when she ate. Then she realized that she was harbouring unforgiveness. She received prayer for this, and her hands were healed. She now could paint beautiful paintings.

Forgive us our debts, as we also have forgiven our debtors.

Simon Wiesenthal (1908–2005) was a Jewish survivor of the Holocaust. Afterwards, he dedicated his life to tracking down Nazi war criminals responsible for the genocide. Wiesenthal wrote a book entitled *The Sunflower: On the Possibilities and Limits of Forgiveness*. In this book, he describes how as a prisoner in a concentration camp during World War 2, he was once ushered into the room of a dying young German SS soldier. Wiesenthal was left alone with the young man who began to tell Wiesenthal of the terrible things he had done to Jewish communities on the Eastern Front in Russia. He spoke for hours. At the end of the time he asked if Wiesenthal, as a Jew, would forgive him. In the book, Wiesenthal asks the reader what he or she would do if they had been in Wiesenthal's place.

Around the time I read that book, the church I was pastoring had a church meeting. In that meeting several people made unfair and unjustified complaints about me and my wife. We experienced a lot of pain and anger about the things people said and what they accused us of. In the weeks after the meeting, it proved very difficult to get beyond the public shaming we had unjustly experienced. We even began to make decisions which would result in being less connected with the very people we were pastoring. We were not in a forgiving mood.

Soon after, I met with a wise and senior Christian leader who was my advisor. At our meeting, he asked what I would like to talk about that day. I said I wanted to talk about Wiesenthal's book and my response and also about a painful church meeting I had experienced. I started with my reflections on Wiesenthal's book. I ended by saying that if I had been Wiesenthal, I would have forgiven the young, dying soldier. Then I began to talk about the church meeting. I described the injustice of the situation and how people had accused us wrongly. I spoke of the public humiliation and how my wife and I were making decisions to put some distance between us and the church we were leading.

My advisor said very little during the time I spoke about the book and then the church meeting. When I finished, he paused and smiled. He asked one question. "Don't you think it strange that you could forgive an SS soldier for genocide, but you can't forgive a church for a meeting?"

Forgive us our debts, as we also have forgiven our debtors.

You might be suffering great injustice in your ministry. You might be suffering anger and grief as you live with cruel words and actions at the hands of others. In the midst of this, you attempt to preach. Listen to the words of Christ from the cross. He speaks a word which sounds beyond the place of the Skull. He speaks a word to his Father for those who do not show concern, awareness or understanding about the pain they cause. The beginning of your journey to forgiveness and abundant life is to allow Jesus's words to be the first spoken. Words spoken to his Father and your Father that you may be able to deeply forgive and know forgiveness.

Forgive us our debts, as we also have forgiven our debtors.

Reflection

Search your heart. What offence are you struggling, or refusing, to forgive someone for?

Pray

Forgive us our debts, as we also have forgiven our debtors.

15

Lead Us Not into Temptation
A Prayer for Preachers Needing Enabling

Luke 23:44–46

> It was now about noon, and darkness came over the whole land until three in the afternoon, for the sun stopped shining. And the curtain of the temple was torn in two. Jesus called out with a loud voice, "Father, into your hands I commit my spirit." When he had said this, he breathed his last.

"For the sun stopped shining" (Luke 23:45). These words sum up the literal and spiritual darkness that cloaked Jesus as he died.

"For the sun stopped shining."

It was noon and the brightest time of day became the darkest time in history. It was as if there was a reversal of creation. The God who said "Let there be light" (Gen 1:3) was now in darkness. The God whose life was the light for all people (John 1:4) was dying in darkness. The God who said "I am the light of the world" (John 8:12) called out into the darkness. The God who breathed the breath of life into humanity was about to breathe his last. The Author of Life (Acts 3:15), through whom all things came into being and are held together (John 1:10; Col 1:16–17), was ending. This short portion of Scripture describes an apparent uncreation.

Hence the words "for the sun stopped shining" describe a terrible reality at several levels.

Jesus cries out with a loud voice from the depths of this darkness. After six hours of such unbearable suffering, you would barely expect that he could whisper. But it is with a loud voice that Jesus calls out of the darkness with words from Psalm 31. Psalm 31 describes a situation where enemies are relentlessly attacking a person. The person in Psalm 31 experiences distress, sorrow, grief, anguish, groaning, affliction and terror. Yet, God is declared as the one who delivers, rescues and is a rock of refuge and strong fortress. As you read Psalm 31, you will notice that the author goes back and forth between declaring God's faithfulness and describing the terror and torment caused by enemies. The part of Psalm 31 Jesus quotes (Ps 31:4–5) speaks of the potential trap that awaits a person. Such a trap threatens the person's life and faith. But in the presence of such a threat there is only one response – committing oneself to God:

> Keep me free from the trap that is set for me,
> for you are my refuge.
> Into your hands I commit my spirit;
> deliver me, LORD, my faithful God. (Ps 31:4–5)

"Keep me free from the trap that is set for me" can be reworded, "Lead us not into temptation." For in difficult and traumatic times, the temptation to stop hoping, stop praying or stop believing is very real. I have often seen strong Christians significantly falter in their faith during times of bereavement or suffering. The temptation to lose trust in God is a real one and is unexpected by many until they are confronted with such a temptation. How much more the need for preachers to be on their guard against such a temptation.

To succumb to this temptation is to walk by your own light in the darkness. In the book of Isaiah there are four portions of Scripture called the "Servant Songs."[1] These portions of Scripture speak of a suffering servant, and Jesus is the fulfilment of these prophetic words. One of the Servant Songs describes the temptation the people face when confronted with darkness. The temptation is to act independently of God instead of trusting God:

> Who among you fears the LORD
> and obeys the word of his servant?
> Let the one who walks in the dark,
> who has no light,
> trust in the name of the LORD
> and rely on their God.
> But now, all you who light fires
> and provide yourselves with flaming torches,
> go, walk in the light of your fires
> and of the torches you have set ablaze.

---

1. Isa 42:1–9; 49:1–7; 50:4–11; 52:13–53:12.

>   This is what you shall receive from my hand:
>   You will lie down in torment. (Isa 50:11–12)

There on the cross, in the darkness, Jesus trusts in the name of the Lord and relies on God. With a loud voice, Jesus calls from Scripture to his Father in this extreme moment. Jesus's cry from the cross provides hope for those times when we feel defeated. In those times when you think you are defeated, when the darkness is great and the temptation to act independently of God is overwhelming, listen to the loud cry of Jesus. Here is a prayer for preachers who are defeated in ministry: "Father, into your hands I commit my spirit."

Listen carefully, remembering the context from which Jesus drew these words (Ps 31) – from the threat of a trap that entices us to act unfaithfully.

Lead us not into temptation.

A preacher writes of a memorable professor who taught her. The professor and his wife suffered the loss of their only child, a son. She describes the deep impact the professor had on her and writes of him, "Out of his great grief, this bereaved father said, 'The Christian life is lived in between – in between My God, my God, why hast thou forsaken me? And Father, into thy hands I commend my spirit.'"[2] She reflects on this:

> So in this . . . saying from the Cross, Luke is teaching us how to die and how to live. Because we, by faith, are assimilated [united] to Christ in his death, we are also assimilated to him in his life beyond death. In his suffering we find our redemption. In his abandonment we find our acceptance. In his dereliction [desolation] we find our salvation. And at last we are able to say even in the midst of doubt and perplexity, *Father into your hands I commend my spirit*, even as the Lord and Savior Jesus Christ said.[3]

The Spirit and Christ intercede for us (Rom 8:26–27, 34) in our defeats and despair. I once had the privilege of hearing Ajith Fernando (Teaching Director for Youth for Christ, Sri Lanka) speak to a gathering of preachers. He mentioned the intercessory ministry of the Holy Spirit in Romans 8:26–27. A "ministry of groaning" is how he termed it. He spoke of the great need for it and how not enough is said about it. He said, "Groaning is an alternative to quitting." I suggest that praying "Lead us not into temptation" is to pray in harmony with the groans of the Spirit of Christ. In those times when you pray "Lead us not into temptation," keep in mind the ministry Jesus has towards us:

---

2. Rutledge, *Seven Last Words*, 77.
3. Rutledge, 77–78.

> For we do not have a high priest who is unable to empathize with our weaknesses, but we have one who has been tempted in every way, just as we are – yet he did not sin. Let us then approach God's throne of grace with confidence, so that we may receive mercy and find grace to help us in our time of need. (Heb 4:15–16)

One day when I was on an extended retreat, things became very dark spiritually. As the day wore on, I discovered that I was unable to pray. It was as if there was a large black curtain before me and light could not penetrate it. I became more distressed as the day went on and I could not make any spiritual breakthrough. I wanted to call out to God, but the words were not there. Finally, in the early evening, a two-word prayer came into my heart: Abba Father. I prayed those words several times, and before me, in the black curtain, a thin split appeared. Light spilled through and poured into my spirit. The darkness was dispelled. I was left with the deep sense that I was benefiting from a Holy Spirit prayer rather than my prayer.

A second incident comes to mind. For most of my life, I have wanted to go on a pilgrimage to the Nazi concentration camp Auschwitz-Birkenau. I wanted to go to pay my respects to the memory of those who had suffered and died there. Eventually, I was able to make my journey, and the day was cold and grey, with a fog shrouding the camp all day. The very weather seemed to mourn this place of evil. Towards the end of the visit, I had fallen behind the group I was with. By the time I arrived at one of the last areas we were viewing, I was alone. This area was a concrete bunker with furnaces where the bodies had been cremated. As I stood there, I realized that this was the place of the first photo I had seen of the Holocaust as a young boy. That was significant for me. I walked out of the bunker but immediately felt directed by God to go back and pray. This seemed the right thing: to stand and prayerfully pay my respects. I re-entered the bunker and stood before the furnaces. But I then realized I could not feel anything whatsoever. I literally could not think, feel, speak or pray. There was nothingness. There was darkness. I was paralyzed. Yet, mysteriously, I felt held and contained by God. Even though I had no thoughts, words or feelings that I could convey to him, I felt held by him. In the nothingness there was Someone. Again, at a time when I was unable to pray, I experienced the intercessory nature of Christ.

While Matthew and Mark record that the temple curtain tore from top to bottom when Jesus gave a loud cry (Matt 27:50–51; Mark 15:37–38), only Luke details what that cry was: "Father, into your hands I commit my spirit." The overall crucifixion led to this majestic moment, symbolizing free access to the

Most Holy Place and the Father's presence. The Father responded specifically to the words recorded by Luke. This leaves us with a vision and a hope for those times when faced with the temptation of giving up as a preacher and disciple. This leaves us with the power and effect of Jesus's words when we are defeated and feeling powerless in the darkness. God is with us.

Lead us not into temptation, and so, Father, into your hands I commit my spirit.

Reflection

In times of darkness, defeat or despair, what temptation do you face?

Pray

Lead us not into temptation.

16

Deliver Us from the Evil One
A Prayer for Preachers Needing Blessing

John 19:30
When he had received the drink, Jesus said, "It is finished." With that, he bowed his head and gave up his spirit.

This last cry from the cross, "It is finished," has several layers of significance. First, the cry announces what is obvious: the moment of Jesus's death. Yet, to only hear the words in this way is to miss words of light in the darkness and words of life in death. These words are not simply marking the time of Jesus's death. These words of Jesus announce the fulfilment of the work of the cross. They are words of a master craftsman. "It is finished" was a common expression spoken by a craftsman upon achieving a project.[1] Here they are uttered by the one who crafted creation and, now, through his work on the cross, crafts a way for people to experience new creation in a fallen world.

The last words of Jesus, "It is finished," announce the achievement of redemption.

Deliver us from the evil one.

Second, they are strong words which announce the deathblow to sin, evil and the kingdom of darkness. With these words, Jesus announces that death no longer has the final word. The writer of Hebrews describes the lasting effect of Jesus's work on the cross: "Since the children have flesh and blood, he too shared in their humanity so that by his death he might break the power of him who holds the power of death – that is, the devil – and free those who all their lives were held in slavery by their fear of death" (Heb 2:14–15).

---

1. Harris, *Seven Sayings*, 77.

The last words of Jesus, "It is finished," announce the death of death.
Deliver us from the evil one.

Third, this cry from the cross is one which resounds loudly. These are not words of resignation and defeat. While the Gospel of John records what Jesus said, the gospels of Matthew and Mark record how Jesus said it: with a loud cry (Matt 27:50; Mark 15:37).

> Since this cry was uttered in a loud voice at the end of Jesus' life, there can be little doubt that it was *a cry of triumph*, not the lament or complaint of a defeated foe. The victim has become the victor.... Significantly, this is the only cry of Jesus on the cross that was not spoken to somebody, but because it was spoken loudly, anyone within earshot could have heard this victorious shout.[2]

The last words of Jesus, "It is finished," announce good news.
Deliver us from the evil one.

Fourth, this cry is a blessing. In describing this cry from the cross, John lists four movements:

1. Jesus *received the drink*
2. Jesus said, *"It is finished"*
3. Jesus *bowed his head*
4. Jesus *gave up his spirit*

John's description echoes the gospel accounts when Jesus distributed bread, such as feeding the multitudes (e.g. Matt 14:19), at the Last Supper (e.g. Matt 26:26) or at the table at Emmaus (Luke 24:30). Jesus would take the bread, bless it, break it, give it. Here, in the final moments on the cross, the same pattern is evident as Jesus offers himself once for all:

1. Take: received the drink
2. Bless: "It is finished"
3. Break: bowed his head
4. Give: gave up his spirit

The last words of Jesus, "It is finished," announce a blessing.
Deliver us from the evil one.

This cry from the cross, "It is finished," continues to sound triumphantly from age to age and in whatever state you find yourself in. Here are words

---

2. Harris, *Seven Sayings*, 79. Emphasis in original.

proclaiming the achievement of full redemption and freedom from the fear of death; words announcing good news and deep blessing from the Saviour. They are words which assure us of the completeness and perfection of Jesus's work on the cross and the life he gives. Jesus's loud cry, "It is finished," drown out the devil's whisper that it is you who is finished. For where there is light, love and life, the evil one attempts to bring darkness, dread and death. To the extent the evil one is successful with this strategy, we are left in discouragement, despair, disillusionment and a soul-chilling night. But from the midst of this night, we hear a cry uttered from the cross: "It is finished." Words we might be saying but with a different meaning and intention than Jesus. For when we say, "It is finished," we have in mind that there is no more life. When Jesus says, "It is finished," he says it as a proclamation that leads to life. Jesus says these words for you and to you. Words which are also said in the hearing of the evil one. Words which speak as loudly today as when Jesus first spoke them.

Deliver us from the evil one.

A passage from the book of Job helps illustrate the power of this cry from the cross. In Job 26, a contrast is made between the whisper of God and the thunder of God. Job begins with a rich description of God's power and knowledge at work throughout creation. Job surveys creation and declares that nothing is outside God's reach or involvement. Even the place of death and destruction lies naked before God (Job 26:6). God's power and presence in creation is both beautiful and frightening. Then Job finishes with this extraordinary summary: "And these [God's work in creation] are but the outer fringe of his works; how faint the whisper we hear of him! Who then can understand the thunder of his power?" (Job 26:14).

According to Job, the tremendous and terrifying displays of God in creation are but the "faint whisper" of God. These are the "outer fringe of his works." Magnificent. Consider the most violent storm you have experienced. Think about the magnitude of mountains, plains and valleys. Look at the night sky and scale of the oceans. These are but the faint whisper of God. These are but the outer fringes of God's work. Job then poses a question: "Who then can understand the thunder of his power?" To put it another way: what if God was really to raise his voice? What would happen if God shouted? What would that sound like?

It sounds like this: It is finished.

The shout of redemption, freedom from death, good news and blessing.

Deliver us from the evil one.

If the works of creation are "but the other fringe of his works" and a "faint . . . whisper," then the centre of God's work is the cross and Jesus's cry is the "thunder of his power." When you preach, regardless of the focus of your message, you are expressing once again all that is contained in the cry "It is finished." You proclaim the centrality of God's work and the power of his voice. You proclaim the completion and perfection of Christ's work on the cross. Whether you preach the Scriptures or hear them preached, take comfort in this word from the cross. For as one writer observes, "It is in the nature of the human being to think that Christ's work could not possibly be finished, that we have to do more, we have to add to it, we have to earn it."[3] Listen again to that cry from the cross and take it to heart: It is finished. Such a word draws people to the centre of God's love and redemption.

When I was eighteen years old, I committed my life to Christ. On the night that happened, the married couple explaining the gospel to me invited me to pray the "sinner's prayer." The "sinner's prayer" involves acknowledging your need for God, asking for his forgiveness and committing your life to him. But when I came to the part of the prayer asking Jesus to forgive my sins, I said to the couple, "I can't ask Jesus to forgive my sins. They are too great." They wisely replied, "Well, just pray what you can." So, I prayed, "Lord, please forgive those sins that you are able to." Of course, that meant he would forgive them all, but I did not realize that at the time. A few months later, I woke one morning with a terrible thought: "You are not really a Christian. You did not pray the 'sinner's prayer' properly. You didn't ask for forgiveness in the right way. You are not a Christian." I got out of bed in a state of shock and despair. I was "finished." I went outside the house and sat at the back door. I was devastated. But not long after I sat there, the father of the family I was living with came and sat by me. I was silent and did not say anything about the awful realization I had woken up to. After a short while, he spoke. He said, "You know. When I became a Christian, I didn't even pray the 'sinner's prayer.'" I looked at him in amazement. The devilish thought that had attacked me fled.

It is finished.

Deliver us from the evil one.

Most people experience times and seasons when the way ahead is shrouded in grey and darkness. There are times when there seems no end or escape to the situation we are in, whether those circumstances were caused by our own sin or through no fault of our own. We feel trapped, and words such as "It is finished" seem like the end and not a beginning. We say "It is finished" by way of a final declaration of our situation rather than hearing Jesus say them by way of a victorious proclamation. Indeed, circumstances are such that we are

---

3. Rutledge, *Seven Last Words*, 63.

afraid words such as "It is finished" mean *"we* are finished." We lose hope that we can be redeemed. We say them as words of death instead of words of life. It is then we most need to hear these words from the cross. It is then we most need to hear Jesus say those words: "It is finished." It is then we most need to hear the "thunder of his power" (Job 26:14).

The shout of redemption, freedom from death, good news and blessing. "It is finished."

Deliver us from the evil one.

In 1968, an English newspaper promoted a round-the-globe yacht race. Competitors had to sail solo and could commence the race anytime between June and October 1968. The race started and finished in England. Whoever sailed the globe in the fastest time would win a handsome cash prize. One of the competitors was a man called Donald Crowhurst. Crowhurst was not experienced at ocean sailing. Sailing was more of a leisure activity for him rather than a profession. However, the prize money was attractive as Crowhurst's business was experiencing financial hardship. Crowhurst commenced the race on 31 October 1968, the last possible day allowed.

Crowhurst's story is complex and tragic. Not long into the race his boat began to give him problems. So Crowhurst made the decision to wait in the South Atlantic Ocean and radio false reports of his progress. He had decided to cheat. Back home there was much excitement as it appeared that Crowhurst was sailing very fast and was likely to win. However, he was literally floating in one area. He also landed in South America to make some repairs to his boat. As the reality of his lies dawned on him, Crowhurst changed his mind. He decided he would re-join the race as the other competitors sailed by his position on their way to the finish line. His plan was to sail behind them and try not to win. He knew if he won his logbook would be studied closely and his deception would be discovered. However, one after another, the other boats either withdrew from the race or sank, apart from one other boat that had already finished. It looked as if Crowhurst might now win with the fastest time. He was totally caught up in a shameful lie.

It is not clear what happened to Crowhurst. But he plunged deeper and deeper into confusion, remorse and despair. His empty boat was found adrift in the Atlantic in July 1969. His last entry in his logbook read in part: "I am what I am and I see the nature of my offence. . . . It is finished. It is finished. IT IS THE MERCY." It remains unclear how Donald Crowhurst lost his life. His wife maintains he never would have taken his own life. I am struck by Crowhurst's final words. No one can be sure if he was drawing on the words of Jesus, but he does speak of his "great God" in his final entry. In a movie about Crowhurst's race, *The Mercy* (2018), one of the final scenes captures the spirit of Jesus's cry from the cross as seen through the tragic story of Donald Crowhurst.

In the movie, people prepare for Crowhurst's triumphant return, and a large banner hangs on the wharf at the finish line. The banner reads: "Welcome home Donald." But when the news breaks that his empty boat has been found adrift, and Crowhurst is missing, one of the scenes is of two people taking down the banner. As they untie the banner, each end of the banner falls, covering the beginning and the end of the message. The scene pauses. The banner has changed in meaning. The message, "Welcome home Donald" now reads "come home." With the change in the message, it struck me as one which now reads more urgently and with a wider invitation. An invitation to all who are losing hope and think they are in an inescapable situation. There is now a spirit of forgiveness and love in the message.

Our Father in heaven longs to say to his children, and all of creation, "Welcome home." Yet, because of sin and evil, we lose sight of home. We lose sight of hope. We lose sight of our Father in heaven. We are lost and say, "It is finished." The cross changes that, and what Jesus cries out changes that. Once and for all. When Jesus says "It is finished," it is with an infinitely deeper meaning and power than when we say it. When Jesus says it, the usual meaning is changed and so is life. When Jesus says it, it carries the urgent and wide invitation, "Come home." He opens the way so the Father can welcome us home. When Jesus says it, he truly delivers us from the evil one.

Reflection

Give thanks for the thunder of God's power, for his words of blessing: "It is finished."

Pray

Deliver us from the evil one.

Part III

The Lord's Prayer as Heard in Jesus's Resurrection

John 20:11–29; 21:1–23

Part III

The Lord's Prayer as Heard in Jesus's Resurrection

John 20:17–29; 21:17–23

17

Our Father in Heaven

A Prayer for Preachers Desiring Revelation

John 20:11–18

Now Mary stood outside the tomb crying. As she wept, she bent over to look into the tomb and saw two angels in white, seated where Jesus' body had been, one at the head and the other at the foot.

They asked her, "Woman, why are you crying?"

"They have taken my Lord away," she said, "and I don't know where they have put him." At this, she turned around and saw Jesus standing there, but she did not realize that it was Jesus.

He asked her, "Woman, why are you crying? Who is it you are looking for?"

Thinking he was the gardener, she said, "Sir, if you have carried him away, tell me where you have put him, and I will get him."

Jesus said to her, "Mary."

She turned toward him and cried out in Aramaic, "Rabboni!" (which means "Teacher").

Jesus said, "Do not hold on to me, for I have not yet ascended to the Father. Go instead to my brothers and tell them, 'I am ascending to my Father and your Father, to my God and your God.'"

Mary Magdalene went to the disciples with the news: "I have seen the Lord!" And she told them that he had said these things to her.

Of all the resurrection stories, this is the one which keeps drawing me back and drawing me in. When I read it, it is as if all Scripture leads to this moment. When I read it, I experience a hush, as if heaven holds its breath as this scene plays out.

The scene is focused on one disciple, Mary. The way Scripture records what happened is tender, beautiful, personal, intimate and yet available to all. Especially for those who have heavy hearts and need to once again – or for the first time – experience the resurrection of Jesus. The events begin on the first day of the week while it was still dark (John 20:1). The first day of the week is dawning and with it, revelation.

Mary's devotion is touching. She goes to the tomb, and unexpectedly, she finds the stone has been removed. She rushes back to tell Peter and John. They run to the tomb and discover that, but for the linen and head cloth, the place where Jesus was laid is empty. Peter and John leave, but Mary remains. She stands by the tomb crying.

The image of this weeping disciple shows that those who love deeply, grieve greatly. The verse "Now Mary stood outside the tomb crying" (John 20:11) communicates much. Her loss is great. Her Lord has died and it seems the body of Jesus has been stolen away. Her grief has deepened terribly. She is confused and there is no one to help. Her sorrow is overwhelming. Her devotion is beautiful.

She knows the tomb is empty but she looks again. What could have possibly changed? Why look again? Sometimes, no matter how bad things are, there can be hope that things might not be what they seem. Weeping, Mary looks into the tomb and into the face of angels (John 20:11–13). However, she is so focused on finding Jesus, she shows no sign of fear – no sign that she even recognizes they are angels. Only one thing matters: she must find the body of Jesus. The angels' question is playful: "Why are you crying?" Why ask a question they know the answer to? You can imagine the angels trying to contain their excitement. By contrast, Mary's answer shows her bewildered sadness. "They have taken my Lord away and I don't know where they have put him" (John 20:13). She assumes "they" are those who crucified him. But this time, "they" have nothing to do with it.

She turns and Jesus is standing there. But he looks like a gardener to her. He too asks the angels' question. But with more detail, "Woman, why are you crying? Who is it you are looking for?" (John 20:15). A little bit more light dawns. Mary thinks maybe he is the one who has carried her Lord away.

These events in John 20 recall the scene from Genesis 3. Humanity in a garden, in distress, and God searching: "Where are you?" (Gen 3:9). John

20 reverses the scene in that first garden where humanity hid and death invaded. Now here in John 20 because of Jesus, humanity is not hiding but searching. Now here in John 20 because of Jesus, death is not invading but life is conquering. Now here in John 20, the Gardener from Genesis 3 is about to answer Mary's request, "Sir, if you have carried him away, tell me where you have put him, and I will get him" (John 20:15).

The dawn brightens.

What happens next is one of the most tender moments in Scripture. One of the most personal and touching. The response Jesus was about to give was not quite like any he had given before. Jesus's response was for Mary then and for all today. This time, Jesus's response was not the commanding assurance he gave on the lake when the disciples thought he was a ghost: "Take courage! It is I. Don't be afraid." (Matt 14:27). This time it was not a statement like the one he gave at a Samaritan well when a woman spoke about the coming Messiah: "I, the one speaking to you – I am he" (John 4:26). No, on this occasion it was different and just one word: "Mary."

Scripture says she turned toward him (had she turned away after his question – frantically looking this way and that for where his body might be?) and cried out, "Rabboni!"

For Mary and the other disciples, the previous days had held horror, trauma, shock and grief. Mary's grief had been worsened by, what she thinks is, the work of grave robbers. Twice now, she has been asked why she is crying. Then her name is spoken by the One she thought she had lost for all time. Her name is spoken. Elsewhere in the resurrection accounts, there are a range of interactions between Jesus and his disciples. For example, Jesus rebukes (Luke 24:25–26); he opens up Scripture (Luke 24:27, 45–49); he invites disciples to touch him to prove he really is alive (Luke 24:39; John 20:27); he performs a miracle (John 21:6); he commissions (Luke 24:46–47; John 21:15–18); and he promises the Holy Spirit (Luke 24:49). But here in John 20, Jesus announces his resurrection by speaking a disciple's name.

It's that simple. It's that personal. It's that beautiful. It's that tender. It's that powerful.

The importance of names in the Bible tumbles into this story of Jesus and Mary. Jesus saying her name recalls the constant theme of people and nations being known by God and called by name: for example, Moses (Exod 33:17); Samuel (1 Sam 3:1–10); Israel (Isa 43:1); the Persian ruler Cyrus (Isa 45:1); and the apostles (Luke 6:12–16). Even the stars do not escape God's careful attention. Each one is named by him:

> Lift up your eyes and look to the heavens:
> Who created all these?
> He who brings out the starry host one by one
> and calls forth each of them by name.
> Because of his great power and mighty strength,
> not one of them is missing. (Isa 40:26)

The practice of God naming continues to the end of the Bible in the book of Revelation. Faithful disciples are promised a new name and are given God's new name (Rev 2:17; 3:12; 14:1). At the end of the age, Christ himself will bear a new name in his ultimate victory (Rev 19:12–16).

Here, at the tomb, in a garden, Mary enjoyed this loving practice of God. Jesus called Mary by name. Jesus called Mary by name into the name of our Father in heaven: "Do not hold on to me, for I have not yet ascended to the Father. Go instead to my brothers and tell them, 'I am ascending to my Father and your Father, to my God and your God'" (John 20:17).

A sister (Mary) is given this message for brothers (the other disciples) about our Father in heaven. God's name, and new family life, is contained in the resurrection message Jesus gave Mary.

God calls you by name. I mean that literally. He calls you by your name and into life in his name.

Our Father in heaven.

"I am ascending to my Father and your Father, to my God and your God."

Perhaps, this resurrection message is one you need to hear in a new way today. You need to hear God address you by name and lead you into a fresh experience of his name.

Our Father in heaven.

You are a preacher. You are familiar with the Scriptures. You know the story of the life, death and resurrection of Jesus. You know what happened and how it ends. You live this side of the resurrection. You live in a privileged time knowing the time and circumstances of the suffering and glories of Christ (1 Pet 1:11). You live knowing what the Old Testament prophets searched diligently for and what angels longed to look into (1 Pet 1:10–12). Yet, life is such that you, too, can find yourself in a similar situation as Mary. You can be, as it were, at the empty tomb early in the morning, while it is still dark, in a state of sadness. You remain devoted to Christ but your sense of him has faded. You are still committed in your faith but you also grieve. You grieve for times and days past when life was brighter and God seemed closer. If angels appeared, they might ask, "Why are you crying?" Mary's words are your words,

"They have taken my Lord away and I don't know where they have put him." For many preachers, there can be days like that. For some, there can be months or even years.

Jesus's question has not lost its intimacy: "Why are you crying? Who is it you are looking for?"

Jesus's response has not lost its power, calling your name and reminding you of what he has done: "I am ascending to my Father and your Father, to my God and your God."

Jesus calls you by name into the name of the Father.

Our Father in heaven.

Mary approached the tomb in darkness and left in light. She approached it seeking Jesus but left with a new message about "Our Father in heaven." She did not expect the resurrection, much less the message that came with it.

Maybe that is the case for you. The idea of hearing your name spoken by God, the idea of being drawn deeper into the name of our Father in heaven, is unexpected. Most things about God breaking into our life are unexpected. Enjoy it! The day is dawning for you.

Our Father in heaven.

As the apostle John would later write, "See what great love the Father has lavished on us, that we should be called children of God! And that is what we are!" (1 John 3:1).

When I was a young adult, the church I attended would give the opportunity for people to speak during the worship service. Anyone who wanted could speak briefly and bring a testimony or talk about a Bible passage. One person who often took this opportunity was an elderly man. However, when he spoke, he would talk too long and not always make sense. He looked and spoke like someone who was absent-minded. Over time he became known for this. So, whenever he went up front to speak, people began to quietly laugh. People were not really listening to him as much as laughing at him. During one evening service, he once again took the opportunity to speak. As usual, he was not making a lot of sense. And, as usual, laughter rippled through the congregation. I remember feeling embarrassed for him. He seemed unaware that people were making fun of him. In a worship service too.

On this occasion he was talking about John 20:11–18, and he focused on Jesus's message to Mary. As he repeated Jesus's words, he emphasized the word "your." He called our attention to it. He slowed his speech. "I am ascending to my Father and *your* Father, to my God and *your* God." He emphasized that sentence and those words. Carefully. Slowly. And as he did, a deep stillness descended upon the congregation. The laughter melted away. People began to listen intently. For me, what he was saying was a revelation. I had not heard this message in this way before. By the silence in the congregation, I was not the only one impacted. That happened many years ago, yet the memory and the message has not faded with time.

I suppose, in a sense, everyone in that worship service had initially mistaken his words for those of a gardener's. That night, we heard our name spoken. That night, we were called into the name of the Father. That night, we heard that the risen Christ had opened the way to "my Father and your Father, to my God and your God."

Our Father in heaven.

Reflection

Be still and close your eyes. Picture yourself in the place of Mary standing at the empty tomb. Hear your name being called.

Pray

Our Father in heaven.

18

Hallowed Be Your Name

A Prayer for Preachers Desiring Faith

John 20:24–29

> Now Thomas (also known as Didymus), one of the Twelve, was not with the disciples when Jesus came. So the other disciples told him, "We have seen the Lord!"
>
> But he said to them, "Unless I see the nail marks in his hands and put my finger where the nails were, and put my hand into his side, I will not believe."
>
> A week later his disciples were in the house again, and Thomas was with them. Though the doors were locked, Jesus came and stood among them and said, "Peace be with you!" Then he said to Thomas, "Put your finger here; see my hands. Reach out your hand and put it into my side. Stop doubting and believe."
>
> Thomas said to him, "My Lord and my God!"
>
> Then Jesus told him, "Because you have seen me, you have believed; blessed are those who have not seen and yet have believed."

Before we examine Thomas's story and failings, we might need to make an honest confession: we preachers can be a disbelieving lot. We believe God but we are not so quick to believe what others say about God. We fail to listen. One reason for this is, as preachers, we are regularly involved in prayer and the ministry of the word. Obviously, praying and studying Scripture is a good thing. However, it becomes a bad thing when we become the master instead of the servant of the word. When we preach, we are in charge. Everyone is listening to our interpretation of the Bible. We can slowly gain a sense of power. The serpent's temptation from the garden of Eden to gain power and be like God rises up (Gen 3:1-4). This temptation is common to all, but for those who preach and pastor, the temptation is worse.[1] We can stop listening to what others say about God. We can become deaf to others. We can become disbelieving.

Along with the sense of power is another potential problem. The more we study the Bible, the more we can become comfortable with the Bible. We can stop listening to it. Our study of the Bible becomes centred on what we will say about it rather than what it is saying to us. This can happen without realizing it. We can become deaf to Scripture. We can become deaf to God. We can become disbelieving.

In the story before us from John 20, Thomas is our representative. He is the disciple who has a commanding presence in the story. His friends tell him the great news that Jesus is alive, but Thomas has questions. He has a list of proofs he needs to see before he will believe. The key thing to realize is that Thomas is not so much disbelieving God, he is disbelieving the community of believers. He does not doubt God; he doubts his friends' testimony about God. He has become disbelieving.

Also, what he requires as proof is gruesome. He will not be satisfied by simply seeing Jesus's wounds; he needs to feel them too. This is a sign of the depth of Thomas's unbelief. He proposes something so dramatic because he does not expect he will need to do it. Also, Thomas's response to the other disciples has the hint of criticism about it. His list of demands is like saying, "Why didn't you require better proof than what you are offering me? I don't want to hear about it; I want to see it. You should have been wiser."

Then a week passes for Thomas and the disciples. You have a group of disciples who have witnessed the risen Christ and one of their number who refuses to believe it. No one likes not being believed. I imagine there could have been frustration, disappointment and anger in that room during that week. It would have been a long week.

Think about how you listen to someone else preaching. Do you listen to what they are saying or how they are saying it? Most preachers I talk to admit they find it difficult to listen to other people's sermons. They find themselves evaluating the sermon rather than absorbing the sermon. They can become deaf to what others are saying about God. In this they are similar to Thomas. They can become deaf to God.

On one occasion, I attended a worship service of a very large church in a major city. Throughout the worship service, I became increasingly upset. In my opinion, there was a significant lack of Bible content in everything,

---

1. Peterson, *Under the Unpredictable Plant*, 12-13.

especially the sermon. I was evaluating it all. At the end of the sermon, the preacher invited anyone who wanted to commit their lives to Christ to come to the front. I could not believe it when I saw numbers of people respond. I sat there thinking, "I do not know who you are committing yourself to because I did not hear Christ preached." I was requiring more proofs than I was seeing. I was Thomas. I was doubting the testimony of my brothers and sisters in Christ. I had become deaf. I had become disbelieving. A few days later I spoke with a wise and senior Christian leader about my deep concerns. He warned me, "Be careful how you judge. The Holy Spirit can work in lots of different and wonderful ways."

Hallowed be your name.

On another occasion I realized I had become too comfortable with the Bible. I had stopped listening to it. As a pastor, I was visiting a young man who was dying of a brain tumour. He was not a Christian. On my third visit I decided to read him a passage from the Bible. His mother, who also was not a Christian, was there. I read 1 Corinthians 15 about the resurrection body and the hope we enjoy in Christ. When I finished reading, I said, "So, what do you think?" His mother, with tears in her eyes said, "Wow. That is good news!" When she said that I was deeply struck with the thought, "She is right. It is good news!" Somehow, I had come to a stage where I treated the good news as old news. I had become deaf. I had become disbelieving. The mother's comment jolted me back to the power of the gospel. The young man committed his life to Christ that day and entered the kingdom. I conducted his funeral a few weeks later.

Hallowed be your name.

This is the challenge for us as preachers – how willing are we to hear God speaking through others?

The picture contained in John 20 can easily be applied to congregations and gatherings of believers. You have a commanding person (usually the preacher) and a community of believers. For reasons given at the beginning of this chapter, the commanding person can become deaf. That person can set certain standards of proof that God is speaking through others and, in the process, miss what God is saying. The image of a locked room (John 20:26) speaks of the culture of such a community. While earlier John 20:19 explains that the doors were locked due to fear of the Jewish leaders, the image of locked doors also describes a spirituality that is closed. Locked doors not only keep people out, they keep people in. Locked doors not only try to control what is happening outside, they try to control what is happening inside. The metaphor of locked doors describes the dangerous spiritual space Thomas was falling into. John Stott writes:

The question of doubt is part of our humanity, it is part of the kind of person that God has made us. Having said that, I would want to illustrate from the story of Thomas. We tend to have sympathy for him, but Jesus didn't. Jesus said to him, "Blessed are those who have not seen but believe," and his position was that Thomas ought to have believed the other apostles, because he knew that they were reliable men and they claimed they had seen the Lord. He had no reason to doubt their claim. Faith rests on testimony – it rests on reliable testimony – and the question to ask ourselves is, "Is the testimony of the apostles in the New Testament reliable?"[2]

As a preacher, are you in such a space? Are you in the place whereby you have stopped listening to others' testimonies and begun to demand proof on your terms? You are in a locked room.

I have deep concerns about a particular book on the Christian market. The book makes bold claims about hearing God speak, and I have many doubts about the method the author describes. I have imagined the challenges I would like to put to the author in the unlikely event I ever met him. One day I was on a short flight between two cities in New Zealand. The woman sitting next to me began chatting to me. She asked me what I had been doing in the city we had flown out of. I explained I had been training pastors. She asked some questions about my work, and I assumed she was not a Christian. I then asked about her. She explained she travelled a lot, especially with her husband. She explained, "He has written a book. So he receives a lot of invitations to speak in churches and at Christian meetings." You can probably guess where this story is going. "What is the name of the book?" I asked. She named the very book I have so many problems with. She began to talk about the book and the circumstances which led her husband to write it. Here was my chance. While she was not the author, she was the next best thing. Now I had my opportunity to present my challenges and doubts. But I could not do it. There was a question in my heart, "God, is she sitting next to me because she needs to hear something from me?" But as the flight continued, I realized my question was wrong. She did not need to hear from me, I needed to hear from her. My concerns about the book did not ease but I was challenged by her grace. The flight was only twenty minutes long yet in that time I saw the difference between her and me. I felt that my attitude was small and mean while hers was warm and friendly. I felt my heart was closed to the possibility that God speaks graciously and spaciously. I felt like I was in a locked room.

---

2. Stott, *Last Word*, 60.

Hallowed be your name.

Fortunately, Jesus can hear through locked doors and just as easily pass through them. In John 20, one week after Thomas outlined what it would take for him to believe the other disciples, Jesus reappears. Jesus shows Thomas his wounds and invites him to place his fingers in the nail marks and his hand in the wound caused by the spear. Jesus stresses the point by saying, "Stop doubting and believe" (John 20:27). Jesus does not commend Thomas's demands for a sign. "Then Jesus told him, 'Because you have seen me, you have believed; blessed are those who have not seen and yet have believed'" (John 20:29). This is one of the messages of the Gospel of John: believe without seeing. Believe without demanding signs and wonders. "It is a better faith that hears and believes rather than sees and believes."[3] Elsewhere, in the Letter to the Hebrews, the faith of many are commended because they believed without receiving what was promised (Heb 11:13, 39–40).

Hallowed be your name.

Thomas unlocks the door of his heart saying, "My Lord and my God!" (John 20:28). Or to put it another way, "Hallowed be your name." This is the challenge for us as preachers. To honour the name of God by dignifying the testimony of those who, by the Holy Spirit, have experienced the resurrected Christ.

"Hallowed be your name" means that God does not need our permission to speak or act in the church's life.

"Hallowed be your name" means that we might need to review our lists of proofs for whether God has spoken or acted.

"Hallowed be your name" means that we might need to listen more and demand less.

"Hallowed be your name" means saying "My Lord and my God" without seeing proofs.

Reflection

Would you describe your heart as a room with a locked or unlocked door? Rather than demanding proof like Thomas, what are others saying about God that you need to listen to?

Pray

Hallowed be your name.

---

3. Carson, *Gospel According to John*, 100.

19

Your Kingdom Come
A Prayer for Preachers Desiring Peace

John 20:19–20

On the evening of that first day of the week, when the disciples were together, with the doors locked for fear of the Jewish leaders, Jesus came and stood among them and said, "Peace be with you!" After he said this, he showed them his hands and side. The disciples were overjoyed when they saw the Lord.

Darkness is falling, the disciples are gathered and afraid, the doors are locked . . . if ever there was a time to pray "Your kingdom come," this was it. The elements of this scene can be symbolically and literally applied to our lives. Life seems to grow darker, our community of faith is fearful, and we do what we can to feel safe. We too pray, "Your kingdom come." We hope and hunger for the kingdom.

But what might it look like if this prayer was answered? What does the kingdom of God breaking into this world look like? What can we expect?

Biblical scholars helpfully describe the kingdom coming as "already but not yet." The kingdom is here in part ("already") and not completely ("but not yet"). The kingdom will fully come when Jesus returns in glory. But what are signs that the kingdom is, in some ways, "already" here? The resurrection story before us (John 20:19–20) helps us see. The opening words of John 20:19 paint a picture which describe the context in which we preach. These words capture the mixture of "already but not yet" in our lives as we pray, "Your kingdom come."

So, let's carefully absorb the words – "On the evening of that first day of the week, when the disciples were together, with the doors locked for fear of the Jewish leaders . . ." (John 20:19) – for these words describe the scene on that first resurrection Sunday and the scene in which we live and preach today.

"On the evening of that first day of the week. . . ."

This phrase holds the sense of anticipation. The verse immediately before this one (John 20:18) records that Mary Magdalene had gone to the disciples with the words, "I have seen the Lord!" She then tells the disciples what Jesus had said to her at the tomb. Peter and John had seen for themselves the tomb was empty (John 20:3–8) but only Mary had seen the resurrected Christ. The disciples have seen a bit and heard a bit, but they have yet to see it all. Now, hours later, it is evening of that same day. They are in a state of anticipation, trying to understand what is happening.

Adding to the sense of anticipation, the words "on the evening of that first day of the week" signal the beginning of a new age. These words have the faint yet distinct rhythm of how the days of creation are counted in Genesis 1. "And there was evening, and there was morning. . . ." We count our days from morning to evening. God counts his days from evening to morning.[1] Or to put it in other ways, darkness then light. Grief then joy. Death then resurrection. Here in John 20, the first day of the new resurrection age is being counted. For us as readers, this adds to our sense of anticipation.

The opening words continue: "When the disciples were together. . . ."

This phrase holds the sense of fellowship. This small community of believers have been through a traumatic time. Many aspects of their life together have ended in violent and shocking ways. Jesus has been brutally killed, Judas has betrayed them all and committed suicide, Peter has denied Jesus and all of them have abandoned Jesus. You could be excused for thinking the story is coming to an end, not a beginning. But we read, "When the disciples were together"; the image of fellowship adds to the sense of anticipation. Together, such anticipation and fellowship position the small community, struck by death, to be resurrected as a community.

The opening of this story continues: "With the doors locked for fear of the Jewish leaders. . . ."

Cold fear is mixed in with the sense of anticipation and fellowship. Yes, something had clearly happened that day which was wondrous. The stories about the risen Jesus and the empty tomb promised that something extraordinary was happening. Yet, there was still the violent threat from those who crucified Jesus. The disciples' fear was well-founded. They were in a city where mob-rule could rise up again and they would be the next ones crucified.

---

1. Meyer, *At the Gates of Dawn*, 101–102.

Fear coloured the anticipation and fellowship. The darkness of evening serves as a metaphor for the fear in their hearts. The disciples had heard news of the resurrection but the defining emotion was fear. There might be comfort in being with each other but it was fear that kept them together in a locked room.

These three elements then – anticipation, fellowship and fear – set up the story for what is about to happen: an encounter with the resurrected Christ. Such a mixture of qualities ought not to surprise us. Throughout the Gospels, Jesus consistently encountered mixed motives and responses to his ministry. He even told parables to highlight such mixed responses. For example, parables such as the parable of the Sower (Mark 4:1–20), the parable of the Prodigal Son (Luke 15:11–32) and the parable of the Two Sons (Matt 21:28–32). This mixture can be summed up by the words of the father who wanted Jesus to heal his son (Mark 9:14–29). When Jesus asked the man if he believed Jesus could heal his son, the father replied, "I do believe; help me overcome my unbelief!" (Mark 9:24).

The mixture of anticipation, fellowship and fear can often be the experience of preachers. They experience anticipation as they prepare the sermon, fellowship as they gather with other disciples to preach it, but also an underlying fear for whatever reason. I know of one preacher who was in a difficult church setting. Over time, a strong-minded group in the church opposed him. When he preached, he removed his glasses so he could not see them shaking their heads in disagreement at his sermon. Sometimes the fear can be because you are preaching in an unfamiliar setting. Or the content of your sermon might be such that you are concerned about the reaction you will receive. Sometimes you might not have any concerns about your sermon but you still are unsure what people might say afterwards. This can create fear.

So, our experience as preachers and as a community of disciples can be a mirror image of the picture in John 20:19–20. There is anticipation, fellowship and fear. The description of being behind locked doors adds to the image. Our faith is comprised of stories of the resurrection, of the need to be with other disciples and of a variety of fears which cause us to gather behind locked doors.

Your kingdom come.

Having looked at ourselves in the mirror of the opening words of John 20:19, we now read, "Jesus came and stood among them and said, 'Peace be with you!'"

"Your kingdom come" finds expression in a locked room.

A locked room marked by fear might seem a small place for a kingdom, but the power of the kingdom tends to be described in small ways. Small ways such as a mustard seed or a small amount of yeast in dough (Matt 13:31–33).

Your kingdom come.

There stands Jesus. He is the fulfilment of the anticipation that had grown during that day; the life of the fellowship of disciples gathered in his name; and the one who speaks peace in the presence of fear.

Your kingdom come.

Yet, there is a mystery here. Having spoken peace to them, Jesus shows his hands and side (John 20:20). Having declared peace, Jesus displays his pain. In the Bible, physical descriptions of people are not that common. In Old Testament stories for example, very little mention is made of someone's physical appearance.[2] So when something is mentioned about their appearance, it is significant, and as readers it is important to take notice. In John 20:20, this dynamic of Scripture is present. The reference to Jesus's hands and side call us to take as much notice as those disciples who were in the room that evening. Jesus shows his wounds as evidence he is the same one who was crucified and who is now alive. I like how, upon seeing the wounds, the disciples' reaction is carefully described: "The disciples were overjoyed when they saw the Lord." The wounds have their place. They have been clearly mentioned for the purpose of confirming that this is the Lord. The text does not read, "The disciples were overjoyed when they saw the wounds." John, the gospel writer, tells of this encounter with the necessary balance and wisdom. He includes the pain of the crucifixion to confirm the wonder of the resurrection. The result is the joyous affirmation of seeing the Lord. Mary's earlier news, "I have seen the Lord" (John 20:18), is echoed. Thomas's later exclamation, "My Lord and my God" (John 20:28), is foreshadowed.

In a context of anticipation, fellowship and fear, Jesus's declaration of peace includes a display of the pain that empowers that peace, which in turn opens the way to joyous recognition of the Lord. Herein lies the mystery. In the presence of anticipation, fellowship and fear, Jesus responds with peace, pain and joy.

All for the purpose of enabling people to recognize the presence of the Lord.

All for the purpose of "Your kingdom come."

Within this mystery is a lesson for preachers. As mentioned earlier, the account of John 20:19–20 describes the contexts we preach into. Places and

---

2. For instance, consider Samson. The only physical feature mentioned is his uncut hair (Judg 13:5). We assume he was powerfully built because he performed great acts of strength. However, if he was so obviously powerfully built, why did Delilah need to plead with him to tell her the source of his strength (Judg 16:4–17)? The secret was he had never cut his hair which was one of the vows of being a Nazirite (Num 6:1–21; Judg 13:4–5). So, apart from his eyes being gouged out, the only physical feature mentioned is his hair.

people full of anticipation, in fellowship and in fear. As we preach, inspired by this story and guided by our Lord, there is a place for preachers to show their wounds.

A saying from the Desert Fathers (around AD 300) makes the observation, "Only the devil disguising himself as Christ has no wounds, being too vain to bear them."[3] There are times in a preaching ministry when it is necessary for a preacher to show others his or her wounds. This involves speaking about those times and events which display vulnerability. For example, times when you have needed to crucify weaknesses and can attest to God's gracious resurrection power in your life. To speak of such times requires humility and courage.

Specifically, such stories of vulnerability can take the following forms:[4]

1. Tension: A story which demonstrates that you too sometimes struggle or have uncertainty in living faithfully for Christ. Such a story can engage the listeners of the sermon. For instance, it might be a story related to an unanswered prayer.

2. Explanation: A story which describes how a biblical truth impacts your life. Such a story can help people understand what a biblical truth means. For instance, it might be a story about experiencing the forgiveness of God.

3. Application: A story which shows how you have tried to live out a biblical truth in your life. Such a story can provide practical examples of how to live in response to the gospel. For instance, it might be a story about how you have tried to tame your tongue.

The purpose of showing your wounds is the same as what happens in John 20:19–20: so that people can see the Lord. Showing your wounds is not for the purpose of making yourself the centre of attention. You might be surprised though by the response of people as you model this practice of Jesus. The people you preach to will appreciate you revealing your heart. You will have shown that, even though a preacher, you are confronted with similar challenges to

---

3. Russ, *Silence*, 98.
4. Hussey and Demond, "Vulnerability in Preaching," 8–9. The authors helpfully add three other ways preachers can talk about their experience. Each option has benefits and dangers. 1. Stories of Success: These can encourage people, but if the successes are overstated then people will be unable to relate to you. 2. Stories of Failure: People will connect with you, but if the failure is a current problem or too confronting people might lose trust in you. 3. Stories of the Journey: These stories can encourage and connect with people, but if the stories are not prepared well they can become shallow observations.

them. You will have shown that you have seen the Lord, and this might help clear their vision.

Your kingdom come.

My wife and I have a dear friend who was a missionary. However, due to some long and difficult situations, she reached the limit of her strength and returned to her home country a broken person. Some years later, we visited her there. We enjoyed a long and leisurely day together. Initially, I was unsure whether to ask about her experiences. But as the day went on, she began to talk about her pain. Within that, there was grief at the loss of the opportunity for ministry and serving Christ. She hungered to return to mission work but her future was uncertain. As the day became evening, possibly even a similar time to that when the events of John 20:19–20 took place, she continued to describe her brokenness. Then she asked, "What does wholeness look like?"

My answer was not my own. I heard myself paraphrase John 20:19–20: "What does wholeness look like? It looks like Jesus still showing the wounds in his hands and side but speaking words of peace and sending others, who were full of fear, out of their locked rooms. It is speaking peace with the wounds still visible."

Your kingdom come.

And may you know the peace that comes from seeing the Lord.

Reflection

What areas of vulnerability in your life might display the grace and presence of the resurrected Christ?

Pray

Your kingdom come.

20

Your Will Be Done on Earth as It Is in Heaven

A Prayer for Preachers Desiring Direction

John 20:21–23

> Again Jesus said, "Peace be with you! As the Father has sent me, I am sending you." And with that he breathed on them and said, "Receive the Holy Spirit. If you forgive anyone's sins, their sins are forgiven; if you do not forgive them, they are not forgiven."

In one sense, the events of John 20:21–23 can simply be read as one thing happening: a commissioning. Jesus announces he is sending the disciples, he breathes on them, and then says, "Receive the Holy Spirit." But it is good if we slow down our reading with this portion of Scripture. It is good if we note the different elements in the story. This scene shows the beautiful impact of Jesus's resurrection.

Jesus's words and actions have three elements: sending, breathing and receiving. When we look at these separate elements, everything turns on Jesus breathing on the disciples. This act is at the intersection of his command ("I am sending you") and his gift ("Receive the Holy Spirit"). To put it another way, the breath of life is given at the point between what God asks us to do and how God empowers us to do it. Jesus's act of breathing on the disciples is like a hinge between the command and the gift. Everything turns on this divine moment.

Your will be done on earth as it is in heaven.

Jesus, who breathed his dying breath on the cross (Mark 15:37; Luke 23:46), now breathes the breath of life into the community of disciples. "Jesus' breathing on his disciples is a reminder of the creative power of the Spirit."[1] This act recalls the great creation moment when the breath of life entered Adam (Gen 2:7). This act recalls the great creation moment when, in a vision to Ezekiel, the breath of life entered dry bones scattered in a valley (Ezek 37:1–14). Now, after the chaos and darkness of the cross, the breath of life is gifted again. Here is a new creation moment.

Like Adam receiving the breath of life, this new act of creation is equally intimate. Such intimacy is seen in that the disciples are surrounded by the Father, Son and Holy Spirit. Jesus speaks words of commission and points to the Father who sent him and the Holy Spirit who comes after him. The disciples are called to life encircled by the presence of Father, Son and Holy Spirit. I like how one biblical scholar describes the shape of such a life: "To the glory of God, through being conformed to the image of the Son, by the empowering of the Spirit."[2] Jesus speaks words sending his disciples and gifting them the Spirit; the breath of life filling their lives. The words of a song entitled "Breathe in Me" captures something of the life-giving need we have for such an encounter with Christ:

> I used to be
> So sensitive
> To the light that leads
> To where you are
>
> Now I've acquired
> These callouses [hardened scars]
> With the darkness of
> A cold and jaded heart
>
> So breathe in me
> I need you now
> I've never felt so dead within
> So breathe in me
> Maybe somehow
> You can breathe new life
> In me again.[3]

---

1. Gine and Cherian, "John," 1446.
2. Fee, *God's Empowering Presence*, 902.
3. "Breathe in Me," by Michael W. Smith and Wayne Kirkpatrick. Copyright © 1995 Deer Valley Music (ASCAP) Universal Music - Brentwood Benson Songs (BMI) Magic Beans Music (BMI) (adm. at CapitolCMGPublishing.com) All rights reserved. Used by permission.

Yet Jesus does not only speak and breathe words of commissioning and gifting; he speaks words which confront his disciples with what could await them. Following his words about receiving the Holy Spirit, Jesus's words in John 20:23 appear harsh: "If you forgive anyone's sins, their sins are forgiven; if you do not forgive them, they are not forgiven." These words describe the nature of the proclamation of the gospel. Some people will respond to the message and others will reject it. The parable of the Sower (Mark 4:1–20) paints a vivid picture of this reality.

But Jesus sends his disciples into such contexts in a distinctive way. Whether they be disciples from John 20 or the twenty-first century, they are sent with a particular quality: "As the Father has sent me, I am sending you" (John 20:21).

Your will be done on earth as it is in heaven.

In John 5:19, Jesus illustrated what it meant for him to be sent by the Father. Jesus said he only did what he saw the Father doing. In that tradition, we are sent to discover God's activity in any given situation and to join in. In the garden of Gethsemane, Jesus prayed exactly that for all believers: "Father, I want those you have given me to be with me where I am, and to see my glory, the glory you have given me because you loved me before the creation of the world" (John 17:24).

How does Jesus's prayer in John 17 compare with the prayers you pray as you are sent to preach? A common preacher's prayer is "Lord, please be with me as I preach this sermon." Yet, in Gethsemane, Jesus prayed just the opposite: he prayed that we would be with him where he is.

As a preacher, you are sent into sermon preparation. From there, you are sent before the people to preach that same sermon. What difference would it make if you engaged in sermon preparation and delivery with Jesus's prayer in mind? "Father, I want those you have given me to be with me where I am, and to see my glory." To do so is to experience being sent in the same manner the Father sent Jesus: going to places and discovering what God is already doing.

Your will be done on earth as it is in heaven.

Over the years, people have sent me their sermons during the preparation phase. They have asked for some guidance and feedback. After some work together, I have often said to the preacher, "Do not do any more preparation on this sermon. It will now be in the telling." The sermon preparation is completed yet there are still gaps. Those gaps cannot be filled with further preparation. It can only be filled or inhabited by the work and presence of God during the actual preaching of the sermon. As a preacher, you cannot predict what that looks like or what fruit will emerge; God is sovereign, and it is *his* word.

God goes ahead of you. It is your task, in being sent to preach in that space, to discern what he has begun. God goes ahead of you. This was one of the features of Jesus's resurrection: those first at the tomb were told he had risen and gone ahead of them. They were to go to where he was and see him there (Matt 28:7; Mark 16:7; Luke 24:6). That kind of resurrection message is a good one to embrace as a preacher every time you preach. In doing so, having been energized with the breath of life, you are sent as the Father sent Jesus.

Your will be done on earth as it is in heaven.

The pastor and author, Eugene Peterson, made a point of conducting his ministry in this way. Wherever he went as a pastor, he did so with this expectation: "I have been anticipated. The risen Christ got there ahead of me. The risen Christ is in that room already. What is He doing? What is He saying? What is going on?"[4] So, for example, Peterson would set off for a hospital visit and recite the message, "He is risen . . . he is going ahead of you to St Joseph's Hospital; there you will see Him, as He told you."[5]

On a trip into south Asia to conduct preaching training, I was especially anxious. It was the first time travelling alone to this region, to a place I had never been, *and* the first time I had experienced a monsoon. So, taking Peterson's lead, I prayed at each stage of the journey, "He has been raised . . . he is going ahead of you to [wherever]; there you will see him, just as he told you." I was operating on the basis that just as Jesus sought to see what the Father was doing, I was seeking to see what Jesus was doing.

When I arrived at the training venue, it was surrounded by a thick forest in a steep hilly area. One day, during a lunch break, I went to the edge of the property and there was a path into the forest and down into a ravine. Two of the course participants were seated on a concrete seat down the path. They walked up and said I should go down there and enjoy the scenery. However, the lunch break was nearly over so I decided to return the next day. So the next lunchtime I walked down the path. No one else was there. Just as I approached the place my friends had been sitting the day before, I noticed another path leading off to the left. I decided to follow it. I walked a short distance through the forest and noticed something in the distance through the trees. I came into a clearing and there, hewn out of the side of the hill, was a tomb – life-size! A large stone was rolled to one side and written on it the words, "Alleluia. He is risen!" In the entrance of the tomb was an image of the risen Christ.

---

4. Peterson, *Under the Unpredictable Plant*, 127–128.
5. Peterson, 127.

The symbolism for this anxious preacher was powerful. Here, in a physical way, God had shown me a spiritual reality. He had gone ahead of me and was waiting for me.

Every time you are sent to study the Scriptures for your sermon, he has gone ahead of you and waits for you.

Every time you are sent and stand to preach that sermon, he has gone ahead of you and waits for you.

Every time.

May you know the breath of life as you study and preach.

May you experience joy as you respond to Jesus sending you and may you see the prayer "Your will be done on earth as it is in heaven" being fulfilled.

Reflection

Receive the breath of life. Into what situation do you think God is sending you? What difference does it make for you to realize that God has gone ahead and is waiting for you?

Pray

Your will be done on earth as it is in heaven.

21

Give Us Today Our Daily Bread
A Prayer for Preachers Desiring Refreshment

John 21:1–14

Afterward Jesus appeared again to his disciples, by the Sea of Galilee. It happened this way: Simon Peter, Thomas (also known as Didymus), Nathanael from Cana in Galilee, the sons of Zebedee, and two other disciples were together. "I'm going out to fish," Simon Peter told them, and they said, "We'll go with you." So they went out and got into the boat, but that night they caught nothing.

Early in the morning, Jesus stood on the shore, but the disciples did not realize that it was Jesus.

He called out to them, "Friends, haven't you any fish?"

"No," they answered.

He said, "Throw your net on the right side of the boat and you will find some." When they did, they were unable to haul the net in because of the large number of fish.

Then the disciple whom Jesus loved said to Peter, "It is the Lord!" As soon as Simon Peter heard him say, "It is the Lord," he wrapped his outer garment around him (for he had taken it off) and jumped into the water. The other disciples followed in the boat, towing the net full of fish, for they were not far from shore, about a hundred yards. When they landed, they saw a fire of burning coals there with fish on it, and some bread.

Jesus said to them, "Bring some of the fish you have just caught." So Simon Peter climbed back into the boat and dragged the net ashore. It was full of large fish, 153, but even with so many the net was not torn. Jesus said to them, "Come and have breakfast." None of the disciples dared ask him, "Who are you?" They knew it was the Lord. Jesus came, took the bread and gave it to them, and did the same with the fish. This was now the third time Jesus appeared to his disciples after he was raised from the dead.

The beginning of this story has the sense of an ending. For the story is centred on Simon Peter at a time when he is empty.

Simon Peter says to the other six disciples present, "I'm going out to fish" (John 21:3). To put Peter's statement in other words, it's as if he says:

> I'm going out to fish. I'm going back to what I know. The past three years have been three years beyond my imagination. I was called by the Messiah to follow him and I witnessed him perform signs and wonders. I heard him teach wonderful things with great authority. I saw him suffer a brutal death and have seen what no one imagined: the resurrected Christ. I have also seen my deep failure. When I was confronted on the night he was arrested, I could not admit I knew him. I lied three times after promising him that I would never fall away. Things seem to have finished now and I think I am finished. I don't see that I have a future as one of Jesus's disciples. Not like it used to be anyway. So, I'm going back to what I know. I'm going out to fish.

So, the beginning of this story seems to signal an ending.

For Peter and others like him who also feel empty: Give us today our daily bread.

There are those preachers who, for various reasons, reach a point when they can no longer continue to preach. They have witnessed the presence of God through the act of preaching and seen fruit from their ministry. However, things are no longer the same.

They are empty.

Give us today our daily bread.

One author outlines four reasons why a person might leave the ministry as a pastor.[1] These reasons can be applied to preachers whether they preach regularly as a pastor or occasionally as a church member.

The four reasons are:

1. Mighty Fall: Usually a moral failing such as wrongful use of money or sexual sin.

---

1. Briggs, *Fail*, 44–47.

2. Tragic Event: Either a personal tragedy or dealing with tragedy affecting others.
3. Slow Leak: The slow and growing effect of dealing with situations which are tiring and wear the person down.
4. Burned Out Statistic: There can be lots of reasons that a person reaches the point of burn-out. Whatever the reasons, the person reaches a stage when they can no longer cope or function in a healthy way.

The first two (Mighty Fall and Tragic Event) are usually obvious. You can easily identify the effects of either of these two events in your life. You would not need someone else to notice them: you will discern the effects easily enough. The other two (Slow Leak and Burned Out Statistic) are not so easy to identify, especially in the early stages. You are unlikely to easily identify the effects of these two events in your life. You would need someone else to notice them: you will not discern the effects easily enough.

I once experienced a combination of the Slow Leak and Burned Out Statistic. After I had been pastoring a church for fifteen years, I needed to deal with a huge crisis in the church. I recognized I was under great stress, but I did not recognize the toll it was taking on me – even though a senior Christian leader I met with regularly wrote to my church leadership expressing deep concern about me. I also failed to recognize my stress despite my heart beating so hard it kept me awake at night.

Several months into the crisis, I travelled to another city to speak at a preaching conference. Friends were shocked at my appearance when I arrived at the conference and immediately sat me down and prayed with me. I was unsure what they were seeing or why they were shocked. However, I recognized I was in trouble thanks to God-ordained conversations throughout the conference. I phoned my wife, Ruth, and told her that when I returned home, we needed to talk and I needed to act. When I arrived home a couple of days later, I described to her what I had discovered about myself. I was unwell and I needed to do something. Ruth replied, "I'm glad to hear you say that because I've already done it." I was confused by her answer. "Done what?" I asked.

She then explained that she had noticed the signs in my life weeks before. She had already contacted various preachers in the city we lived and had arranged guest preachers to minister during our Sunday worship services. I would not be preaching for three months! I was shocked.

I protested, "But you can't do that!"

She replied, "What were you just saying? That you needed to do something? Well, I've already done it."

So, for the next three months I did not preach. I led worship in our church services and every week someone else preached. I was worried that someone in the leadership or the congregation would notice the change and complain. However, no one said a word about it. Without God's intervention through others, I had come close to not being able to preach for a long time, if ever again.

I was empty.

Give us today our daily bread.

For those preachers who are empty and starving for the intervention of God, Peter provides a picture of what God can do.

As if to highlight his emptiness, when Peter goes out to fish, he experiences an empty night of fishing. He and the others catch nothing (John 21:3). But in response to such emptiness, towards the end of the story is the simple message of Jesus, "Come and have breakfast" (John 21:12). This invitation to a meal is also the heart of the story.

Give us today our daily bread.

Jesus feeds Peter and the disciples physically and spiritually. In doing so, they are repositioned to continue the adventure with and in Christ. The feeding takes place by way of reminders and re-enactments of events from the previous three years with Jesus. The echoes and reminders of events from the previous three years revive these weary souls.

Jesus's command to throw out the nets again (John 21:6) echoes Peter's first encounter with Jesus in Luke 5:1–11. Then, on the Sea of Galilee, as now in John 21, Peter had been fishing all night without success. Jesus told him to throw the nets out again, and Peter and his companions were overwhelmed by the size of the catch.

The catch in John 21:11 is described as 153 large fish, but surprisingly, the nets do not break. When the same miracle had taken place in Luke 5:6, the nets had begun to break, and the boats began to sink. Maybe the mention that the nets did not break on this most recent occasion was itself a tender message to Peter that all would be well.

Give us today our daily bread.

When the miraculous catch happened, "The disciple whom Jesus loved said to Peter, 'It is the Lord!'" (John 21:7). Peter wrapped his outer garment around him, and immediately jumped into the water to make his way to Jesus. This is in contrast to the miraculous catch of fish in Luke 5, when Peter fell at Jesus's knees and asked Jesus to depart from him because he was a sinful man (Luke 5:8).

Give us today our daily bread.

And so it goes on. The story contains a number of moments which could well have brought much to mind for those there that day. Those who were empty were now being sustained by the presence, acts and words of Jesus.

For there was a fire again (John 21:9), just like in the courtyard where Peter denied Jesus (Luke 22:55). There was the presence of fish and bread (John 21:13) which could have brought to mind those times Jesus fed thousands with the same food items (John 6:1–15). There was Jesus taking the bread and giving it to them (John 21:13), which echoes his actions at the Last Supper (Matt 26:26).

There is the comment that "None of the disciples dared ask him, 'Who are you?' They knew it was the Lord" (John 21:12). Perhaps a reflection of the great question and answers given at Caesarea Philippi when Jesus asked, "Who do people say I am?" (Mark 8:27–30).

The famous twentieth-century Rabbi, Abraham Joshua Heschel, observed that the Old Testament can be summed up in one word: remember. That observation holds true for the New Testament and for our Christian faith.[2] We are fed by such memories and re-enactments.

Give us today our daily bread.

I once attended a Bible conference where Tom Wright[3] was the main speaker. During one of his talks, he said something which was not in his prepared notes. It was as if the thought came to him suddenly, and he spoke it with deep passion. In fact, it is the only thing I remember about the conference.

He said, "You have to tell people the Story. Every week when they gather for worship tell them the Story. They forget. So you must tell them the Story every week." There is that kind of thing happening here in John 21 – disciples who are experiencing emptiness are being reminded of the Story of God. They are being reminded of their place in the Story. They are being fed by reminders and re-enactments.

Indeed, is this not the task of preaching – to help people recall the works and wonders of God? Is this not the task of preaching – to hold up the

---

2. For example, every time we celebrate the Lord's Supper, we are engaged in an act of remembering. "For I received from the Lord what I also passed on to you: The Lord Jesus, on the night he was betrayed, took bread, and when he had given thanks, he broke it and said, 'This is my body, which is for you; do this in remembrance of me.' In the same way, after supper he took the cup, saying, 'This cup is the new covenant in my blood; do this, whenever you drink it, in remembrance of me.'" (1 Cor 11:23–25).

3. Tom Wright (or N. T. Wright) is a highly esteemed New Testament scholar and theologian. He is a retired Anglican bishop and the author of many books and Bible commentaries.

emblems of faith and point to key markers on the Way? Is this not the task of preaching – to empower people to experience God and, in so doing, receive their daily bread?

Yet, to preach in such a manner, preachers who are empty and are about to go out fishing are invited to hear the word of Jesus, "Come and have breakfast."

What is God trying to remind you of? He wants to feed you.

Give us today our daily bread.

Reflection

What is God trying to remind you of from your earlier days as a disciple?

Pray

Give us today our daily bread.

22

Forgive Us Our Debts as We Also Have Forgiven Our Debtors
A Prayer for Preachers Desiring Kindness

John 21:15–17

When they had finished eating, Jesus said to Simon Peter, "Simon son of John, do you love me more than these?"

"Yes, Lord," he said, "you know that I love you."

Jesus said, "Feed my lambs."

Again Jesus said, "Simon son of John, do you love me?"

He answered, "Yes, Lord, you know that I love you."

Jesus said, "Take care of my sheep."

The third time he said to him, "Simon son of John, do you love me?"

Peter was hurt because Jesus asked him the third time, "Do you love me?" He said, "Lord, you know all things; you know that I love you."

Jesus said, "Feed my sheep."

It has been observed that we are not content in being right until we have proven the other person quite wrong. While this is not true of everyone, all the time, I suspect it is true of most people some of the time. Especially when we have been wronged, and our sense of justice demands evidence that the other person realizes their offence. Naturally, there is a place for confession of wrongdoing when someone has caused harm (e.g. Jas 5:16; 1 John 1:9). However, when it is obvious that someone is aware of their actions, how much more do we require of them?

Forgive us our debts, as we also have forgiven our debtors.

The spirit by which we are forgiven is as important as what we are forgiven for. One of the most powerful examples of this is the image of the father in the parable of the Prodigal Son (Luke 15:11–32). The Prodigal Son decides to return home and plans what he will say to his father. He intends to acknowledge his sin. He will bargain with his father so that he will be welcomed by him; he will say that he is no longer worthy to be called a son, so he will be a hired servant instead. However, as the son approaches his home, his father sees him in the distance. The father rushes to him full of compassion. The son begins to give his prepared confession but his father interrupts him. Instead, he is restored as a son and clothed accordingly. The remarkable thing is *how* the father forgave. He did not remind his son of his wrongdoing or require a long explanation. We see the same kind of forgiveness in the story in John 21:15–17. If there was ever a time when someone was justified in rehearsing someone else's sin while extending forgiveness, this was it. But Jesus acts with the same kindness as the father in the parable he told.

We know the background well enough. On the night Jesus was arrested, Peter declares he is ready to die for him. Jesus instead predicts the opposite: he says that by the time the rooster crows at dawn, Peter will have denied him three times. All four gospels record the heart-wrenching event.[1]

Now, in John 21:15–17, sinner and Saviour are again together. John writes that this is the third time the resurrected Jesus appeared to his disciples (John 21:14). I wonder how Peter felt on the previous two occasions. I wonder if Peter dreaded the possibility that Jesus would mention his denial or whether he wanted Jesus to say something just to get it over with. Jesus shows the perfect balance between both options. Jesus's way of forgiving is marked with kindness.

Forgive us our debts, as we also have forgiven our debtors.

Bible commentators make the point that Jesus's three questions to Peter are cancelling out his three denials. Yet Peter is hurt when Jesus asks if he loves him the third time (John 21:17). Surgery hurts. Even when performed with gentle kindness. Three times Peter's reply contains the words "You know that I love you" and, the third time, "You know all things." Jesus indeed "knows all things"; he not only predicted Peter's fall, he had also predicted Peter's restoration. It is unclear if Peter recalled the restoration part. On the night of Jesus's arrest, he said to Peter: "Simon, Simon, Satan has asked to sift all of you as wheat. But I

---

1. Matt 26:31–35, 69–75; Mark 14:27–31, 66–72; Luke 22:31–34, 54–62; John 13:36–38; 18:15–18, 25–27.

have prayed for you, Simon, that your faith may not fail. And when you have turned back, strengthen your brothers" (Luke 22:31-32).

The sifting had happened. Jesus's prayer had been fulfilled. Peter's faith was still intact. He was still in the presence of Jesus. He had turned back. Now it was time to strengthen others. Or in the words of Jesus: "Feed my lambs"; "Take care of my sheep"; "Feed my sheep."

Forgive us our debts, as we also have forgiven our debtors.

Like the story from John 21, there may be something you do not want to talk with Jesus about. You know Jesus sees and knows all. However, you are not sure if you can bear to have a conversation about it. The memory is too shameful. You are caught between never wanting to recall it and feeling the need to talk it through. Maybe, like the Prodigal Son you have rehearsed what you will say when seeking forgiveness. Maybe, like the Prodigal Son you have decided you will bargain with God to be welcomed back.

The situation of Peter in John 21:15-17 is more common than we might realize. People are burdened by an obvious failing but to speak of it is to relive it. To speak of it is to run the risk of being overcome by it again. So they try to bury it.

Some years ago, I attended a retreat at a ministry centre in a peaceful wooded area in a major city of over one million people. The person leading the retreat said he wanted me to get up early one morning to see the sunrise. I chose the day, but when I woke up, I realized that I did not have long until the sun rose. However, because the retreat centre was surrounded by tall trees, I needed to drive ten minutes to reach a hill to see the rising sun over the horizon. I quickly drove to the hill, and just as I reached the top, the horizon started to change colour. The sky became blood-red and looked angry. I got out of the car and stood watching. I was just in time. I was not prepared for what I was about to experience.

Before and below me was the sprawling city. The sun appeared, and its light began to strike the city. The sunlight spread across buildings, homes and streets. But it wasn't the sight that was extraordinary; it was the sound. Roosters. As the sun raced across the city and replaced the shadows, wherever the sun hit, roosters crowed. I was astounded. Roosters! This was not the type of city I associated with roosters. Yet, in that moment, I sensed God speaking. Peter hearing a rooster crow on that dreadful night immediately came to mind. Here the same principle was being played out. People were waking to the sound of roosters mocking them and reminding them of their failures. I sensed God saying that people were waking to the daily reminder of their broken promises and acts of betrayal. Even betrayal of God himself. They faced another day of carrying the memory of what they had done; another day of experiencing a lack of peace deep in their heart.

Forgive us our debts, as we also have forgiven our debtors.

In John 21:15-17, we see the kindness of God. Kindness which is full of gentleness, generosity and graciousness. Just what is needed for anyone haunted by past sin and failings, unsure if they can speak of it again. Even though the memory of it whispers in their soul ceaselessly. Souls which desperately need to experience the kindness of God.

The kindness of God accessed through the prayerful words of "Forgive us our debts, as we also have forgiven our debtors."

Words which are especially apt for those who preach the Scriptures.

Words which are especially apt for those who preach the Scriptures and are unsure if they can bear having a conversation with God. Unsure if they can bear having a conversation about that secret failing that crowing roosters mock and remind them of.

Words which are especially apt for those who preach the Scriptures and need to experience the kindness of God.

Words which are especially apt for those who preach the Scriptures and need to experience "Forgive us our debts, as we also have forgiven our debtors."

After three years in pastoral ministry, I decided to go on a guided seven-day silent retreat. I had never been on a silent retreat, but somehow my soul hungered for that kind of space. The daily routine was prayer and reading in silence except for a one-hour meeting with the retreat director to discern what God was saying. I was not in a good spiritual state going into the retreat. I had been working too long, too hard, and I was empty. My prayer life was very poor. As the time for the retreat drew near, I was certain of one thing: what God would say. I knew when I was in a place of silence and prayer, God would speak about my lack of prayer. That much was certain. I was dreading it and expecting it. So, I prayed in preparation, "Lord, I know what you are going to say. My only request is that you make it quick so that the pain is short-lived." I was in the dilemma of not wanting to talk about it but realizing it needed to be talked about.

The retreat began and, on the first day, as expected, God spoke. However, what was unexpected was what he said. He used a gospel text to say he loved me. I was caught off-guard. I thanked God for his love but waited for the expected rebuke about my prayerlessness in ministry. A day or two passed. Through further prayer, reading and discussion with the retreat leader, God's first word to me was repeated. He restated his love for me. More days passed and I fearfully waited for the inevitable challenge about my prayerlessness in ministry. It never came. Instead, time after time, God spoke about his love for me. I was astounded. I know what I would have said to someone like me if I was God, but thankfully, I am not God! So, as the week progressed, the message about God's love deepened and expanded. God never spoke about my lack of prayer; only of his love. The result? I discovered I was praying a lot more.

Forgive us our debts, as we also have forgiven our debtors.

Reflection

What conversation does Jesus want to have with you so he can show you the kindness of his forgiveness?

Pray

Forgive us our debts, as we also have forgiven our debtors.

23

And Lead Us Not into Temptation
A Prayer for Preachers Desiring Perseverance

John 21:18–19

"Very truly I tell you, when you were younger you dressed yourself and went where you wanted; but when you are old you will stretch out your hands, and someone else will dress you and lead you where you do not want to go." Jesus said this to indicate the kind of death by which Peter would glorify God. Then he said to him, "Follow me!"

Of the Twelve disciples, Peter is unique. While Jesus predicted general future events concerning the other eleven (for example, Judas's betrayal and all of them falling away when Jesus was arrested), his predictions about Peter are particularly detailed.

Jesus predicted Peter's unfaithfulness. He not only predicted that Peter would deny him, he predicted it would be three times and before dawn. Here, in John 21, Jesus predicts Peter's faithfulness. He predicts the kind of death Peter would suffer to glorify God.

This prediction about Peter's faithfulness is made just after Jesus reinstated Peter as a result of his unfaithfulness (John 21:15–17). Peter is at a crossroad, and Jesus's words in John 21:18–19 illustrate that. The words are both clear and mysterious. Peter is at a stage of life where Jesus can point back to when Peter was young and point forward to when he will be old. Jesus points back to when Peter was in charge and points forward to when others will take charge. This signals to Peter that he is at a crossroad between life in the past and life in the future.

Within Jesus's message, there is an important phrase on which the prediction turns: "You will stretch out your hands" (John 21:18). At the time of Jesus, this phrase meant crucifixion. John, the gospel writer, wants the reader to understand this. So he writes, "Jesus said this to indicate the kind of death by which Peter would glorify God" (John 21:19). Then Jesus finishes by restating his call to Peter, "Follow me" (John 21:19).

At its simplest, these verses state a spiritual truth to Peter and all who read them: if you walk the way of the cross, it will mean suffering then glory. There is no other way. To help our understanding, this message can be reworded as it relates to us. You will recognize other parts of Scripture in this paraphrase:

> There was a time when you decided what you wanted to do and where you wanted to go. But I call you to deny yourself, take up your cross and follow me. In this world you will have trouble. But take heart! I have overcome the world. I will lead you, and as you mature in your faith, I will increase, and you will decrease. In this you will glorify our Father in heaven.

This is especially important for preachers to understand. To live or preach otherwise is to potentially communicate a kind of discipleship which is not according to the Scriptures.

Suffering then glory.

This pattern is seen most clearly in Jesus's life. He says to the two disciples on the road to Emmaus, "How foolish you are, and how slow to believe all that the prophets have spoken! Did not the Messiah have to suffer these things and then enter his glory?" (Luke 24:25–26). We see it as a constant theme in the life and writings of Paul. For example, "Now if we are children, then we are heirs – heirs of God and co-heirs with Christ, if indeed we share in his sufferings in order that we may also share in his glory" (Rom 8:17).

The temptation is to attempt to keep control of our lives. One of the common ways we succumb to this temptation is to resist any suggestion of hardship and suffering for the sake of the gospel. The temptation is to seek glory without suffering. It is no accident that this was one of the temptations Satan presented to Jesus in the desert (Luke 4:5–7). It is no accident that preachers can also be tempted in this way. The preaching ministry has a place of prominence among God's people and we expect their attention when we preach. If we do not guard ourselves, such a ministry can give us ideas of glory rather than suffering.

Lead us not into temptation.

Jesus's words to Peter were fulfilled about thirty years later. Peter was martyred under the rule of the Roman Emperor Nero around AD 64.[1] One of the gifts Peter left us was his words contained in 1 and 2 Peter. In those letters we can see that Peter lived faithfully beyond the day that Jesus spoke the words contained in John 21. In particular, we see that Peter took to heart the message that the pattern of Christian discipleship is suffering then glory.

In his two letters, Peter writes to Christians who are under pressure and persecution. Towards the end of his first letter, he addresses the elders of the church. Notice the pattern of suffering then glory:

> To the elders among you, I appeal as a fellow elder and a witness of Christ's sufferings who also will share in the glory to be revealed: Be shepherds of God's flock that is under your care, watching over them – not because you must, but because you are willing, as God wants you to be; not pursuing dishonest gain, but eager to serve; not lording it over those entrusted to you, but being examples to the flock. And when the Chief Shepherd appears, you will receive the crown of glory that will never fade away. (1 Pet 5:1–4)

Then in his second letter, he begins by calling the church to grow in their knowledge of Jesus Christ and to guard against stumbling. Then Peter shows he never forgot Jesus's words on the shore of the Sea of Galilee. Having exhorted his readers to live godly lives, Peter speaks of his death:

> So I will always remind you of these things, even though you know them and are firmly established in the truth you now have. I think it is right to refresh your memory as long as I live in the tent of this body, because I know that I will soon put it aside, as our Lord Jesus Christ has made clear to me. And I will make every effort to see that after my departure you will always be able to remember these things. (2 Pet 1:12–15)

These are the words of someone who is at peace with how Jesus is leading him, even though it is towards his death. These are the words of someone who learned not to succumb to the temptation of avoiding the pattern of Christian discipleship: suffering then glory.

As a preacher, test whether you have succumbed to the temptation to avoid the pattern of suffering then glory. Consider your last ten or fifteen sermons; what clear themes emerge? If people were to live in accordance with these

---

1. Gine and Cherian, "John," 1448.

sermons, what would their discipleship look like? If apostle Peter listened to your preaching, what would his response be to how you speak of suffering and glory? Would he live according to the gospel you preach?

In the city where I pastored for a number of years, there was a pastor who had led his church for over thirty years. He said to me, "You will face the consequences of your preaching after seven years." He was referring to a regular preaching ministry to the same congregation. He believed that after seven years you would see the fruit of your preaching. I discovered that was true in my setting. In John 1:17, it states that grace and truth came through Jesus. After seven years, I realized my preaching emphasized grace rather than grace and truth. My preaching needed both. I could see the effect on the discipleship of some of those I was preaching to. I needed to make changes.

What kind of disciples is your preaching forming in relation to suffering and glory? What kind of example do you set for those watching your life? Can they discern the biblical pattern of discipleship: suffering then glory?

Lead us not into temptation.

I can think of someone who models this kind of discipleship. I was at a Langham preaching event in a south Asian country. One night, as we prayed for each other, one of the participants requested prayer for an ongoing situation. He was an indigenous Christian who served as a missionary in a difficult region of his country. He told us this story.

He encountered a woman who was not a Christian but a believer of another major religion. She suffered from an illness which meant she had no energy. She did not even have the strength to lift the smallest weight. The participant said he prayed for her and she was miraculously healed. As a result, she committed her life to Christ. However, her husband was in the military and, at that time, was on a posting far from home. He was a powerfully built man and also a powerful figure in village life. When he returned home, he discovered that his wife was healed and was now a Christian. He dragged her by her hair up to the roof of their house. He threw her down before the household idol and said, "Spit the name of Christ!" She replied, "How can I? He healed me." So he beat her, threw her in a locked room and vowed to kill the missionary. While telling us this story, the missionary displayed gentleness and humility. He was not seeking prayer for his life but for the life of the man and woman. One of the other participants in the group must have recognized the look of astonishment on my face. By contrast, they, as citizens of that country, were not astonished. They were aware of such stories. The participant simply said to me, "The region he ministers in is called 'the graveyard of missionaries.' It is known as being a hard place."

A few months later, I returned for another Langham preaching seminar and asked the missionary if the husband had tried to cause him harm. He said, "Not yet." He explained that the husband continued to make threats, so the missionary decided to visit him. When he arrived at the family home, the father of the healed woman was there to meet him. The father honoured him greatly and hosted him generously. The man was so grateful his daughter was well again. The husband, however, did not enter the room or show himself at all. With compassion, the missionary said he was still praying for this man's conversion and was seeking any opportunity to lead him to Christ. I was astounded at his humility and courage. Here was a preacher and disciple who lived the pattern of discipleship described to Peter on the shore of the Sea of Galilee.

Later, the missionary sent an email to a group of us to say the Christians in his area were under persecution. Churches were being burned and pastors were being beaten up during Sunday worship services. One of his friends took three months to recover from a beating he received. The missionary requested prayer as they were arranging a peaceful march in response to the attacks. As someone who has not experienced anything remotely close to such persecution, I was in awe of the faith expressed. My admiration deepened further when one of those in that country replied to the original email rejoicing, "Let's praise God because surely a 'Saul of Tarsus' will emerge from this persecution."

Suffering then glory.

Lead us not into the temptation of believing it is glory without suffering.

Reflection

In what ways do you seek glory and avoid suffering for the gospel?

Pray

Lead us not into temptation.

24

Deliver Us from the Evil One
A Prayer for Preachers Desiring Vision

John 21:20-23

Peter turned and saw that the disciple whom Jesus loved was following them. (This was the one who had leaned back against Jesus at the supper and had said, "Lord, who is going to betray you?") When Peter saw him, he asked, "Lord, what about him?"

Jesus answered, "If I want him to remain alive until I return, what is that to you? You must follow me."

Because of this, the rumor spread among the believers that this disciple would not die. But Jesus did not say that he would not die; he only said, "If I want him to remain alive until I return, what is that to you?"

The preferred way for a story to end is with things coming to a place of rest and resolution. The earlier twists and tension of the story are settled. All is well. How much more so, then, with the gospels? After the events of Jesus's ministry, suffering and crucifixion, how fitting to end the story with his resurrection and ascension. How apt to finish with the presence of the resurrected Christ, the news still sinking in and the promise of what God will do next.

Matthew finishes his gospel on a mountain with Jesus calling the disciples to an expanded life (Matt 28:16–20). We settle into the scene knowing that we have a part in what happens next.

Mark's gospel finishes with the beautiful words of an angel sitting in the empty tomb. His message is tender, exhilarating, incredible and reassuring

(Mark 16:6–8). Even so, the women are left bewildered and afraid. We smile at the scene knowing what happens next.

Luke finishes his gospel with the promise of power from on high, the ascension, joyful worship and praise (Luke 24:45–53). We sing along with the scene knowing we are part of what happens next.

That leaves one gospel ending: John's. In contrast to the other gospels, his ending is messy. We squirm at the scene, knowing we are prone to repeat what happens next.

John speaks about a rumour circulating among the believers: John will remain alive until Jesus's return. John describes the event that gave birth to the rumour. At first glance it seems nothing more than an embarrassing moment for Peter.

Peter had just been commissioned to care for Jesus's flock, counselled about his future and called to follow Christ (John 21:15–19). So far so good. But then Peter turned and saw that John was also following. So, he asked, "Lord, what about him?" (John 21:21). Jesus gave Peter a blunt answer, "If I want him to remain alive until I return, what is that to you? You must follow me" (John 21:22). This is a rebuke and most of us would cringe if we were on the receiving end of it. Most of us could repeat Peter's mistake and ask Jesus the same question, "Lord, what about . . . ?" We probably would deservedly receive a similar reply. "Jesus' answer was a rebuke to Peter and all disciples."[1]

However, this story is more than just about a misguided question; this is about the threat of evil. Look again at the wording from this biblical passage: "Peter turned and saw that the disciple whom Jesus loved was following them. (This was the one who had leaned back against Jesus at the supper and had said, 'Lord, who is going to betray you?') When Peter saw him, he asked, 'Lord, what about him?'"

What is striking is that John recalls what happened at the Last Supper. When Jesus said one of the Twelve would betray him, Peter motioned to John to ask Jesus which disciple he meant (John 13:23–25). We know who the betrayer was. But of all the events in Jesus's life, why does John recall this one in John 21? Why introduce the language of betrayal now? Is John suggesting there is the possibility of a repeat?

At the Last Supper, Peter and John worked together to ask who was going to betray Jesus. This time it seems they are working against each other. At the Last Supper it could be any one of twelve; this time it is one of two. At the Last Supper, John was clear about the influence of Satan (John 13:26–27). "As soon

---

1. Gine and Cherian, "John," 1448.

as Judas took the bread, Satan entered into him. So Jesus told him, 'What you are about to do, do quickly'" (John 13:27). John summed up the visible and invisible evil using four words, "And it was night" (John 13:30). Darkness had descended on the day and into the heart. Here, in John 21, the resurrected Christ speaks, calls and leads. The light of the resurrection beckons. Peter hears, obeys and follows. But the night of evil threatens again.

Deliver us from the evil one.

This portion of Scripture, at the end of the Gospel of John, demonstrates this incident is an important matter. This event impacted the community of believers. The spirit in which we speak to others about others is not without effect.

Deliver us from the evil one.

The presence of Satan is often hidden in plain sight, but it is eventually made obvious. Where Satan has a foothold, our response to the purposes of God are obstructed. Rumours within the church hold the seeds of confusion and conflict.

Deliver us from the evil one.

After pastoring a church for seventeen years, in my final sermon I spoke of leaving with one regret. I regretted not recognizing evil at work within the congregation quickly enough. As I reflected, it occurred to me that "evil" is "live" spelled backwards. And "devil" is "lived" spelled backwards. If you want to discern the presence of evil within the community, look for a reversal of gospel life. Where there ought to be forgiveness, there is bitterness. Where there ought to be peace, there is anger. Where there ought to be faith, there is anxiety. Where there ought to be unity, there are rumours. Where there ought to be obedience to God, there are questions such as "Lord, what about him?" or "Lord, what about her?"

This last story in John 21 exposes a desire of our hearts. A craving. We all want what someone else has. Fear and anxiety rise within, and we are afraid of missing out. We want to be sure we have the best deal being offered. This has been a problem since the serpent deceived Adam and Eve into thinking God was not offering all he could (Gen 3:1–6). So the questions lurk in our hearts: "What about him?"; "Why does she seem to have more than me?"; "Is there more?"

To satisfy this greed is to betray the call on your life and God who called you.

Deliver us from the evil one.

Preachers have more reason than most to be vigilant about this. Preaching is a prominent ministry. You stand, you preach, people listen. All attention is on you. To preach is both a delight and a danger. To preach is to stand in a place of power; pride can sneak into your soul. Pride and greed will cause you to see other preachers as rivals in Christ rather than relatives in Christ. You will have difficulty celebrating their effectiveness. One nineteenth-century pastor's words still apply today: "Never envy a popular preacher. This is, unhappily, one of the besetting sins of our profession."[2] He added to remember always that the one "whom you would not choose as your pastor is doing a world of good to multitudes you could never reach."[3]

This besetting sin of preachers crouches at your door, and you must master it. Resentment and jealousy can so easily consume us. We see this in the life of King Saul (1 Sam 18:6–11). Admittedly, this is a dramatic comparison. But such was King Saul's jealousy of the young shepherd-warrior David that Saul was driven to obsessed madness. The biblical text describes Saul's simmering anger, obsessive thoughts and destructive self-talk, along with the presence of evil and the hurling of spears. Clearly, we are not going to descend to those depths, but you alone know the secret thoughts that plague you when you consider someone as your rival. You alone know the thoughts that lodge in your heart like fishhooks. You alone, and God. And he sees the spears you hurl. "Lord, what about him? What about her?"

Deliver us from the evil one.

Consider the occasions the apostle Paul encountered this. He had jealous rivals in the churches wherever he went (e.g. 2 Cor 10–12:10; Gal 1:6–9; Phil 1:15–18), yet he remained focused on Christ and the preaching of the gospel. Paul showed astonishing grace in seeing beyond it all and rejoicing in what truly matters:

> It is true that some preach Christ out of envy and rivalry, but others out of goodwill. The latter do so out of love, knowing that I am put here for the defense of the gospel. The former preach Christ out of selfish ambition, not sincerely, supposing that they can stir up trouble for me while I am in chains. But what does it matter? The important thing is that in every way, whether from false motives or true, Christ is preached. And because of this I rejoice. (Phil 1:15–18)

May we be inspired by a story often told about the two great English preachers of the eighteenth century, John Wesley and George Whitefield:

---

2. Wilcox, *Pastor Amidst His Flock*, 166.
3. Wilcox, 166.

It is a matter of historic record that the two great English evangelists, John Wesley and George Whitefield, disagreed on doctrinal matters. Both of them were very successful, preaching to thousands of people and seeing multitudes come to Christ. It is reported that somebody asked Wesley if he expected to see Whitefield in heaven, and the evangelist replied, "No, I do not."

"Then you do not think Whitefield is a converted man?"

"Of course he is a converted man!" Wesley said. "But I do not expect to see him in heaven – because he will be so close to the throne of God and I so far away that I will not be able to see him."[4]

No spears being hurled there!

You preach because of the word and work of God in your life. Where and when you preach is because of the will of God and the willingness of people to listen to you. Jesus has said to you "follow me," and your preaching ministry is part of your response.

Are you content in that? Or to borrow the language of the prophet Zechariah, "Do you despise the day of small things?" (Zech 4:10). Do you have ambition to preach to larger gatherings? To become more widely known.

The pastor and writer, Eugene Peterson, touches on this:

> Several times when my place seemed inadequate for my vision of what I wanted to do for God, a story held me fast to my place, the story of Gregory of Nyssa, who lived in Cappadocia in the fourth century. His older brother Basil, a bishop, arranged for his brother to be appointed bishop of the small, obscure, and decidedly unimportant town of Nyssa. Gregory objected; he didn't want to be stuck in an out-of-the-way place. His brother told him that he didn't want Gregory to obtain distinction from his church but rather to confer distinction upon it. Gregory went where he was placed. And he stayed there. The preaching and writing that he did in that backwater community continues its invigorating influence to this day.[5]

On his deathbed, a famous rabbi named Zusia (1718–1800) wept. He said, "When I face the celestial tribunal [God], I shall not be asked why I was not Abraham, Jacob or Moses. I shall be asked why I was not Zusia."[6] He was

---

4. Wiersbe, *Be Joyful*, 44.
5. Peterson, *Christ Plays*, 73–74.
6. Wiesel, *Souls on Fire*, 120.

grieving about the possibility that he had not lived according to God's call or as the person God had created him to be.

Maybe you need what Peter received on the day John 21 describes. After the incident that we have been focusing on, Jesus intensified the call, "You must follow me" (John 21:22). Have you turned your attention away from Jesus and looked at this or that person? You have been asking the Lord about his plans for them rather than his plans for you. Maybe the only answer you are going to get is a strong reminder of God's call, "What is that to you? You must follow me."

One of the best ways to hear that call again is to pray "Deliver us from the evil one."

Reflection

Is there someone whose ministry you envy? Listen to Jesus's words: "What is that to you? You must follow me."

Pray

Deliver us from the evil one.

Epilogue

This book began with the story about the QANTAS pilot, Captain Richard de Crespigny, and how he safely landed a crippled aircraft saving the lives of over 460 passengers and crew. His story was an example of how good formation and foundation in his life empowered him to act courageously and competently in a crisis. However, that plane very nearly did not land safely. Crespigny describes how his co-pilot saved them from a fatal mistake.

The co-pilot on that flight was First Officer Matt Hicks. During the inflight emergency it was his job to read aloud all the emergency checklists while the flight crew made adjustments to keep the plane in the air. He read out over one hundred checklists, and as they prepared to land, his voice was nearly gone and he was mentally exhausted. Just before they approached Changi Airport (Singapore) to land, Crespigny turned his attention to making a long announcement to the passengers while Hicks took the controls and flew the plane. There were two other captains on the flight deck throughout this emergency. At this point, those two captains were calculating the safe landing speed for this wounded aircraft. They were using a computer programme. They advised Hicks of the landing speed. Crespigny describes what happened next:

> I rejoined the crew just as performance information for our landing was coming forward from Dave and Harry [the other two captains]. I heard Matt being asked to enter the approach speed of 145 knots. . . . With his left hand, Matt started keying buttons, then he stopped and thought. His eyes rose up to the left looking through me in a daze, and then he said: "It can't be 145 knots – it's far too slow!"
>
> Matt was right. At 145 knots . . . we wouldn't stay in the air, we would stall. . . . Matt was 100 per cent [correct]. After a long hour of actioning . . . checklists, and with a hoarse voice and a tired mind, he still had enough mental space, thought and common sense to catch what the rest of us had missed. Pilots make mistakes and they cannot process data as fast as a computer. But pilots have *judgement*. It was a brilliant moment from Matt.[1]

---

1. Crespigny, *QF32*, 229–230. Emphasis in original.

This co-pilot, a junior pilot on the flight deck, questioned the judgement of two captains and a computer. He saved the lives of the passengers and crew in doing so. First Officer Hicks's background story is not described in the book about this flight emergency, *QF32*. I wonder what formation and foundation had taken place during his life that led to that "brilliant moment"? His place in the story enriches and expands the story. His place in the story unexpectedly opens it up in a way that invites more reflection and wondering.

As does your story within this world. Your story may not be widely known, but it is known by our Father in heaven. And your story in Christ can unexpectedly open up new spaces that lead to life for others.

I wonder what formation and foundation is taking place in your life by the work of the Spirit and the effect of the Lord's Prayer. As you prayerfully and slowly engage with the Lord's Prayer, I wonder what gifts and graces within you are being honed by the loving work of God. I wonder what kind of preacher you are being formed into and where you are being called to.

I wonder what works of salvation and redemption Christ wants to involve you in through preaching as you embrace his prayer and serve his world.

As you have listened to the Lord's Prayer through Jesus's life, death and resurrection, the Lord's Prayer has begun to echo in your life for others to hear. The sound of the Lord's Prayer grows ever louder.

> Our Father in heaven,
> hallowed be your name,
> your kingdom come,
> your will be done,
> on earth as it is in heaven.
> Give us today our daily bread.
> And forgive us our debts,
> as we also have forgiven our debtors.
> And lead us not into temptation,
> but deliver us from the evil one.

Bibliography

Bailey, Kenneth E. *Finding the Lost: Cultural Keys to Luke 15*. St. Louis: Concordia Publishing House, 1992.

Briggs, J. R. *Fail: Finding Hope and Grace in the Midst of Ministry Failure*. Downers Grove: InterVarsity Press, 2014.

Carson, Don. *The Gospel According to John*. Leicester: Inter-Varsity, 1991.

Crespigny, Richard de. *QF32*. Sydney: Pan Macmillan, 2012.

Fee, Gordon D. *God's Empowering Presence: The Holy Spirit in the Letters of Paul*. Peabody: Hendrickson, 1994.

Fee, Gordon D., and Douglas Stuart. *How to Read the Bible for All Its Worth*. 4th ed. Grand Rapids: Zondervan, 2014.

Gine, Pratap C., and Jacob Cherian. "John." In *South Asia Bible Commentary: A One-Volume Commentary on the Whole Bible*, edited by Brian Wintle, 1386–1448. Rajasthan: Open Door, 2015.

Green, Joel B. *The Gospel of Luke*. NICNT. Grand Rapids: Eerdmans, 1987.

Harris, Murray. *The Seven Sayings of Jesus on the Cross: Their Circumstances and Meaning*. Eugene: Cascade, 2016.

Heschel, Abraham. *I Asked for Wonder: A Spiritual Anthology*. Edited by Samuel H. Dresner. New York: Crossroad, 2010.

Hussey, Ian, and Alan Demond. "Vulnerability in Preaching: How Far Is Not Far Enough?" *Journal of the Evangelical Homiletics Society* 18, no. 2 (September 2018): 5–20.

Johnson, Darrell W. *Fifty-Seven Words that Change the World: A Journey Through the Lord's Prayer*. Vancouver: Regent College Publishing, 2005.

Keener, Craig S. *A Commentary on the Gospel of Matthew*. Grand Rapids: Eerdmans, 1999.

Kunst, Judith M. *The Burning Word: A Christian Encounter with Jewish Midrash*. Brewster: Paraclete Press, 2006.

Larsen, David L. *The Anatomy of Preaching: Identifying the Issues in Preaching Today*. Grand Rapids: Baker, 1989.

Marcus, Joel. *Mark 8–16*. Anchor Yale Bible. New Haven: Yale University Press, 2009.

Meyer, F. B. *At the Gates of Dawn*. London: Kingsgate Press, 1910.

Morris, Leon. *Luke*. Tyndale New Testament Commentary. London: IVP, 1974.

Nieman, James R. "Preaching that Drives People from the Church." In *A Reader on Preaching: Making Connections*, edited by David Day, Jeff Astley, and Leslie J. Francis, 247–254. Aldershot: Ashgate, 2005.

Peterson, Eugene. *Christ Plays in Ten Thousand Places*. London: Hodder & Stoughton, 2005.

———. *Under the Unpredictable Plant: An Exploration in Vocational Holiness*. Grand Rapids: Eerdmans, 1992.

Robinson, George. *Essential Judaism: A Complete Guide to Beliefs, Customs, and Rituals*. New York: Atria, 2000.

Ross, Maggie. *Silence: A User's Guide*. Vol. 1, *Process*. London: Cascade, 2014.

Rutledge, Fleming. *The Seven Last Words from the Cross*. Grand Rapids: Eerdmans, 2005.

Scaer, David P. *The Sermon on the Mount: The Church's First Statement of the Gospel*. St Louis: Concordia, 2000.

Simon, Arthur. *How Much Is Enough? Hungering for God in an Affluent Culture*. Grand Rapids: Baker Books, 2003.

Stewart, James S. *Heralds of God*. New York: Charles Scribner's Sons, 1946.

Stott, John. *The Last Word: Reflections on a Lifetime of Preaching*. Milton Keyes: Authentic Media, 2008.

———. *Sermon on the Mount*. Downers Grove: InterVarsity Press, 2000.

Takatemjen. "Luke." In *South Asia Bible Commentary: A One-Volume Commentary on the Whole Bible*, edited by Brian Wintle, 1327–1385. Rajasthan: Open Door, 2015.

Tozer, A. W. *The Knowledge of the Holy*. Bromley: OM Publishing, 1987.

Wiersbe, Warren. *Be Joyful (Philippians): Even When Things Go Wrong, You Can Have Joy*. 2nd ed. Colorado Springs: David C. Cook, 2008.

Wiesel, Elie. *Souls on Fire: Portraits and Legends of Hasidic Masters*. New York: Simon & Schuster, 1972.

Wilcox, G. B. *The Pastor Amidst His Flock*. New York: American Tract Soc., 1890.

Langham Literature and its imprints are a ministry of Langham Partnership.

Langham Partnership is a global fellowship working in pursuit of the vision God entrusted to its founder John Stott –

> **to facilitate the growth of the church in maturity and Christ-likeness through raising the standards of biblical preaching and teaching.**

Our vision is to see churches in the Majority World equipped for mission and growing to maturity in Christ through the ministry of pastors and leaders who believe, teach and live by the word of God.

Our mission is to strengthen the ministry of the word of God through:
- nurturing national movements for biblical preaching
- fostering the creation and distribution of evangelical literature
- enhancing evangelical theological education

especially in countries where churches are under-resourced.

Our ministry

Langham Preaching partners with national leaders to nurture indigenous biblical preaching movements for pastors and lay preachers all around the world. With the support of a team of trainers from many countries, a multi-level programme of seminars provides practical training, and is followed by a programme for training local facilitators. Local preachers' groups and national and regional networks ensure continuity and ongoing development, seeking to build vigorous movements committed to Bible exposition.

Langham Literature provides Majority World preachers, scholars and seminary libraries with evangelical books and electronic resources through publishing and distribution, grants and discounts. The programme also fosters the creation of indigenous evangelical books in many languages, through writer's grants, strengthening local evangelical publishing houses, and investment in major regional literature projects, such as one volume Bible commentaries like *The Africa Bible Commentary* and *The South Asia Bible Commentary*.

Langham Scholars provides financial support for evangelical doctoral students from the Majority World so that, when they return home, they may train pastors and other Christian leaders with sound, biblical and theological teaching. This programme equips those who equip others. Langham Scholars also works in partnership with Majority World seminaries in strengthening evangelical theological education. A growing number of Langham Scholars study in high quality doctoral programmes in the Majority World itself. As well as teaching the next generation of pastors, graduated Langham Scholars exercise significant influence through their writing and leadership.

To learn more about Langham Partnership and the work we do visit **langham.org**